BASIC MANAGEMENT SKILL AND ENERGY MANAGEMENT

CHANDAN M

PES COLLEGE OF ENGINEERING

MANDYA -571401

Shri. K S Vijay Anand President, People Education TrustMandyaWe are grateful to PET (People Education Trust), the president of our unbearable organization, for their encouragement and support of this book.

P E S College of Engineering, Mandya, Karnataka, India.

Contents

Authors Profile

Mr.CHANDAN M

The author is pursuing a Bachelor of Engineering in the Department of Electrical and Electronics Engineering at PES College of Engineering, Mandya. He is an accomplished researcher who has published several research papers in peer-reviewed journals with high indexing quality and patents, and he is passionate about research in UV technology, organic semiconductors, and superhydrophobic surface modification. He is also passionate about the fields of marketing, entrepreneurship, and business management. He has participated and won awards in many business pitching competitions.

Authors Profile

JAGADISH V K

The author is pursuing a Bachelor of Engineering in the Department of Electrical and Electronics Engineering at PES College of Engineering, Mandya. He is an accomplished researcher who has published several research papers in peer-reviewed journals with high-indexing qualityand patents. He is also passionate about research in shape memory alloys, Organic semiconductors, and superhydrophobic. He has two years of industry experience in L&T and KMS Coach body builder Pvt ltd. and has attended many business pitching competitions.

Authors Profile

NANDAN V H

The author is pursuing a Bachelor of Engineering in the Department of Electrical and Electronics Engineering at PES College of Engineering, Mandya. He is an accomplished researcher who has published several research papers in peer-reviewed journals with high indexing quality and patents. He is also passionate about research in piezo electric material, shape memory alloys , Organic semiconductors, and superhydrophobic. He is also passionate about the fields of marketing, enterprinal activity and business management. He has attended many business pitching and Shark Tank competitions.

Acknowledgements

We would like to acknowledge and express our gratitude to many of our instructors and colleagues, whose constructive feedback allowed me to improve the book's content and have it published.

Throughout my life, I am thankful for the support and guidance of **my parents** for helping me to focus on positivity and passion. Thank you for everything

I want to express my gratitude to **Mr. Nandan V. H. and Mr. Jagadish V K,** the co-authors, for their efforts on the whole work. Their encouragement and hard work motivated me to complete the book. We really appreciate their assistance and prompt support.

I would like to thank the management of **P. E. S. College of Engineering in Mandya**, Karnataka, India, for their valuable suggestions, constant encouragement, and support during this project. We really appreciate their assistance and support.

I would like to thank the whole faculty of the **Department of Electrical and Electronics Engineering** at the **P. E. S. College of Engineering in Mandya**, Karnataka, India, for their support in helping me complete my book.

I'd like to thank Professors **Siddesh Kumar N M and Ramesh Kurbet** of the **Mechanical Engineering Department at P.E.S. College of Engineering in Mandya,** Karnataka, India, for their assistance in seeing my book through to completion.

I would like to special thank to Professor and Head of the Department, **D M Srinivasa** of the Department of Electrical and Electronics Engineering at the **P. E. S. College of Engineering in Mandya**, Karnataka, India, for their support and guidance in helping to my successful journey.

I thank my friends **SURAJ R, BHEEMKUMAR HALOOR,** and **VIJAYKUMAR R** for helping me to focus on this work

There is no such thing as a flawless human being. On the exam, there were undoubtedly a few mistakes. Readers will be compensated for their involvement in the book's production if they provide helpful suggestions and constructive criticism to increase its usefulness.

CHAPTER I

Introduction to Management Skills

1.1 Management: The act of organizing people to achieve desired goals and objectives while effectively and efficiently employing the resources at hand is management.

Various Skills: Hard talents are more akin to what one may find on a CV. i.e., training, experience, and degree of proficiency. The non-technical, intangible, personality-specific abilities that define one's qualities as a leader, listener, negotiator, and conflict mediator are known as soft skills. In other words, it refers to characteristics like personality traits, social grace, linguistic skills, personal routines, friendliness, and optimism that distinguish persons to varying degrees.

1.2 Soft skills include

- **Interpersonal skills:** These include the ability to lead, motivate and delegate. It is used by a person to interact with other people.
- **Team working:** Co-operation between those who are working on a task. Teamwork is generally understood as the willingness of a group of people to work together to achieve a common aim.
- **Negotiation skills: Negotiation** is a conversation between two or more people or parties intended to reach a beneficial outcome over one or more issues. This beneficial outcome can be for all of the parties involved, or just for one or some of them.
- **Communication skills:** The ability to convey information or share ideas with another effectively and efficiently
- **Time management:** It is the process of organizing and planning how much of time you spend on specific activities.
- **Stress management:** It is various methodologies to control a person's level of **stress**, especially chronic **stress**, usually for the purpose of improving everyday functioning.
- **Interpersonal skills:** Interpersonal skills include being able to lead, inspire, and delegate. It is used by a person to communicate with others.

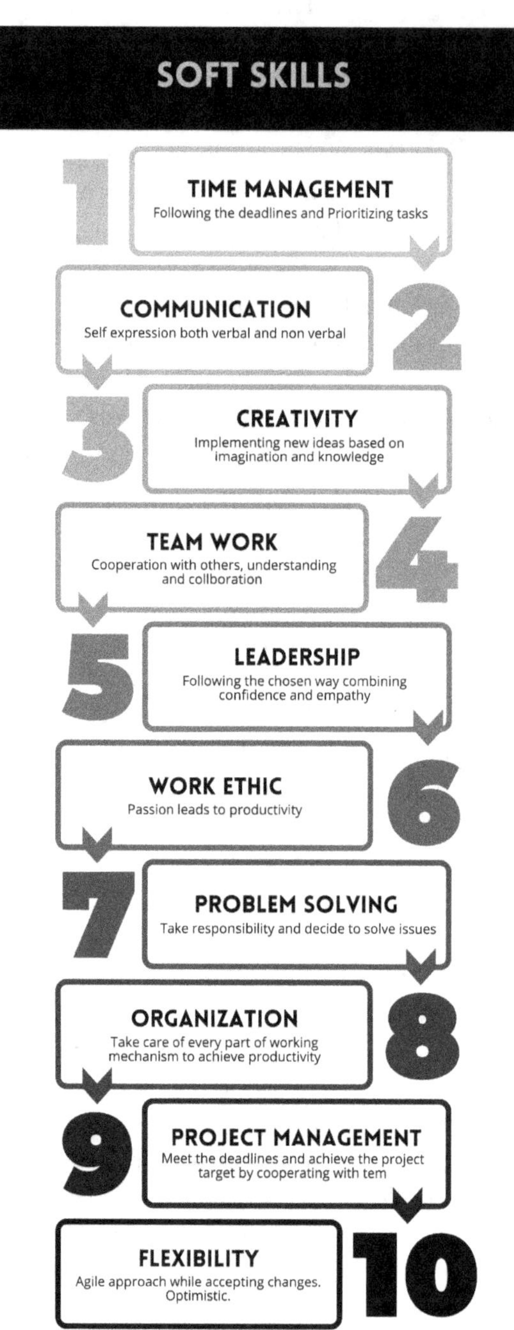
SOFT SKILLS
1
TIME MANAGEMENT
Following the deadlines and Prioritizing tasks
2
COMMUNICATION
Self expression both verbal and non verbal
3
CREATIVITY
Implementing new ideas based on
imagination and knowledge
4
TEAM WORK
Cooperation with others, understanding
and collboration
5
LEADERSHIP
Following the chosen way combining
confidence and empathy
6
WORK ETHIC
Passion leads to productivity
7
PROBLEM SOLVING
Take responsibility and decide to solve issues
8
ORGANIZATION
Take care of every part of working
mechanism to achieve productivity
9
PROJECT MANAGEMENT
Meet the deadlines and achieve the project
target by cooperating with tem
10
FLEXIBILITY
Agile approach while accepting changes.
Optimistic.

- **Teamworking:** Teamwork is the collaboration of people who are engaged in a job. Teamwork is often defined as a group of people's desire to work together to accomplish a shared goal.
- **Negotiation skills: Negotiation:** A negotiation skill is a dialogue between two or more people or parties with the goal of reaching an agreement on one or more topics. This advantageous conclusion may benefit all of the people involved or just one or a few of them.
- **Communication skills:** the ability to transmit information or thoughts to another person in an effective and efficient manner.
- **Time management:** Time management is the practice of arranging and planning how much time you devote to different tasks.
- **Stress management: It** refers to a variety of methods for controlling a person's level of stress, particularly chronic stress, with the goal of enhancing daily functioning.

1.3 Process of knowing yourself

- Understand your own talents and shortcomings, as well as your likes and dislikes.
- Be conscious of your emotions, feelings, and responses to what is going on around you.
- Recognize how these moods and emotions affect your mental condition.
- Examine your interactions with others.
- Examine how your surroundings affect you.
- Keep a personal journal to convey your emotions such as likes, dislikes, interests, and so on.
- Meditation may help you achieve mental tranquility.
- Exercise on a regular basis to maintain physical and mental strength and health.
- Regular walks are a kind of moving meditation.
- Create new hobbies and interests.
- Do some riding or driving to help you discover a calm spot.
- Make some trips just for fun, such as a picnic or a relaxing spot.

1.4 Importance of knowing yourself :

Knowing yourself is a life-long process. Understanding and knowing ourselves is very important in our lives and help us develop good relations with everyone. You must know yourself in order to be useful to yourself and others. Thus it helps

- to control emotions
- to reach our goal
- to reach better decisions
- to improve relationship
- to realize and improve your full potential
- to experience happiness and joy
- to lead our life in a better way
- to improve our personality
- to become more competent and accepted by others
- to change our attitudes and improve our values

1.5 SWOT Analysis:

Strengths

- barbering is a skill that is always in demand
- People enjoy barbering as it is a social experience.

Weaknesses

- expand their business by opening more locations
- offer more services such as hair styling or shaving.

Opportunities

- barber shops can be expensive
- some people fear barber shops.

Threats

- offer more services such as hair styling or shaving.
- the rising cost of rent or lease prices.

SWOT is an acronym for "Strength, Weakness, Opportunity, and Threat. SWOT analysis may be utilized for personal development as well as organizational development. SWOT Analysis is an effective tool for identifying your strengths and weaknesses, as well as opportunities and threats. A SWOT analysis is a business tool that helps you discover the positives and negatives inside your firm (S-W) and outside of it, in the external environment (O-T). Developing a complete understanding of your position may aid in both strategic planning and decision-making.

1.6 Benefits of SWOT analysis

- It can be scaled.
- The people taking part find it easy. They can readily understand the ideas and procedures.
- Both an individual and a business level may practice it.
- less costly.
- Being inclusive enables for team engagement, and the outcomes are more likely to reflect actual surroundings.

	Positive factors	Negative factors
Internal factors	Strengths	Weaknesses
External factors	Opportunities	Threats

SWOT Analysis Grid: A SWOT Analysis uses a grid of four squares as shown below.

Strengths:

- What are you good at?
- What resources are available to you that is pertinent?
- What qualities do others think you possess?
- What skill do you possess that no one else does?

- What exclusive or inexpensive resources can you access that no one else can?
- What is your backbone of you?

Weaknesses:

- What would you change?
- What missteps do you make?
- What must you keep away from?

Opportunities:

- What worthwhile possibilities are available to you?
- What intriguing trends do you know about?
- How can you seize chances from your strengths?

Threats

- What challenges do you encounter?
- What are your rivals up to?
- Is your job at risk due to evolving technology?
- Do you have issues with bad debt or cash flow?
- what is the problem you are facing?

Performing this analysis will often be instructive - both in terms of highlighting what needs to be done and in terms of putting issues into perspective.

1.6.1 Usage of SWOT Analysis

A powerful technique for analyzing environmental data and information is the SWOT analysis, which considers both internal (strengths, weaknesses) and external (opportunities, threats) elements. It is beneficial to reduce the impact of your company's deficiencies while promoting its strengths.

Finding the positive and negative characteristics and modifying them as necessary is helpful. Be honest about your strengths and weaknesses while utilizing the SWOT analysis, and be explicit in reference to the current circumstances. Avoid complexity and keep your SWOT analysis brief and straightforward.

1.7 How to Do a SWOT Analysis

1.8 Perception

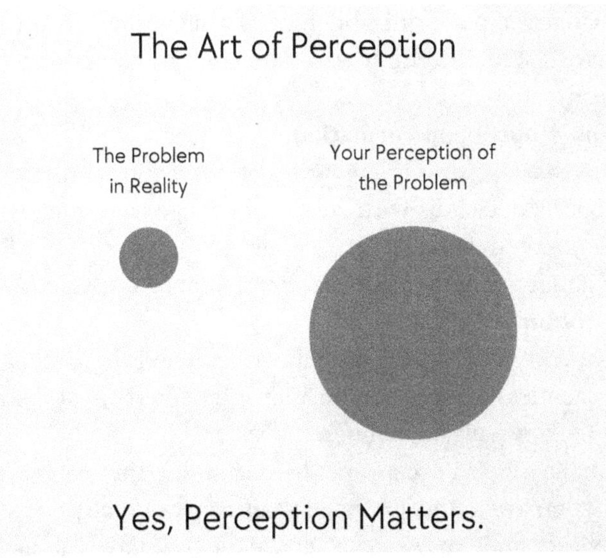

perception: The ability to see, hear or become aware of something through the senses

1.8.1 Strategies for Improving Perception

There are seven important strategies for improving perceptual skills, i.e,

1. Knowing Oneself Accurately
2. Be empathetic
3. Having a Positive Attitude
4. Positive/Postpone Impression Formation
5. Open communication
6. Comparing One's Perception with that of Others
7. Improving Diversity Management Programs.

1. Knowing Oneself Accurately:

Regular interactions with peers and open, honest conversations with others can aid in improving understanding.

2. Be Empathetic:

The capacity to comprehend and pay attention to the emotions of others is referred to as empathy. Empathy is a natural phenomenon that appears in people on its own.

3. Have a Positive Attitude:

Attitudes have a powerful and long-lasting influence on perception. When we have a bad attitude toward someone or something, our view is certain to be affected.

4. Postpone Impression Formation:

Do not reach a decision on anything or someone with just one or two meetings. Making decisions with scant knowledge is extremely dangerous. A far better method is to delay making an impression until additional information about the person and the circumstance is gathered.

5. Open Communicating:

Due to a communication breakdown, perception becomes warped. Ensure that the message reaches the appropriate person, at the appropriate time, and in the appropriate manner.

6. Comparing One's Perceptions with that of Others:

Through comparing and exchanging ideas, we come across alternative points of view and may as a consequence have a much deeper understanding of the situation and the issue.

7. Introducing Diversity Management Programs:

An essential method is to employ training programs that might assist in expressing the benefits of diversity to people from diverse backgrounds.

1.9 Communication

Communication is the process of transfer of information from sender to receiver, with the information being understood by the receiver.

1.9.1 Communication process

Communication is the process of transmitting information and understanding from one person to another.

- Noise- It is defined as any disturbance that interferes with communication.
- Feedback-Feedback is the recipient's response; without it, the sender cannot know if the full message was viewed.
- Sender - The communication process begins with the sender, who transmits a message to the recipient.
- Message - It might be a concept, data, or information that the sender sends to the recipient.
- Encoding- Encoding is the process of converting a message into a symbolic form.

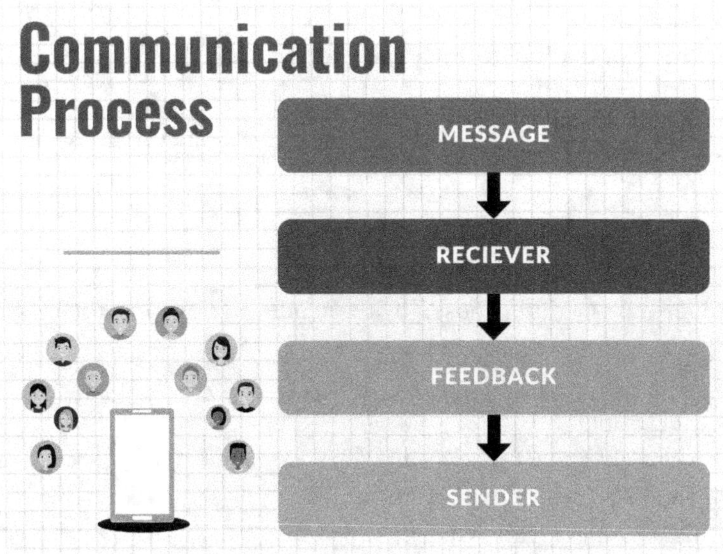

- Channel- The medium via which the communication passes is referred to as the channel.
- Receiver- The individual to whom the message is to be delivered.
- Decoding - At the receiver's end, the encoded message is retranslated to get the original message

1.9.2 Special Features of Communication

- Communication is a two-way traffic
- Communication is unavoidable.
- Communication is a social process.
- Communication is a continuous process.
- Communication is universal.

1.9.3 Channels of Communication

Channel- The medium chosen by the sender to transport the message to the recipient. Channels of communication are

- Upward channel
- Downward channel(directive channel)
- Horizontal channel or diagonal channel
- Informal channel (grape wine)

Upward channel:

Information from a lower level to a higher level, such as suggestions and complaints

Downward channel (directive channel):

Information from the top level to the lower level like instruction, directions, motivation, etc.,

Horizontal channel or diagonal channel:

Communication among lower-level people without consulting their superiors or communication among equals.

Informal channel (grape wine):

- Misleading information and rumors which is always undesirable
- Possibly avoid this channel for communication.

Some more channels are

- Telephone
- Radio
- Television
- Newsletter
- Postcard
- Magazine articles
- Newspaper columns
- Mobile Fax and Internet

Formal communication network:

It is intended by management to govern communication flows in order to eliminate confusion and make them more organized, timely, and seamless. Formal communication about firm direction and instruction travels downhill from executives to directors to managers to personnel. Formal communication in the form of data and reports travels upward from workers to managers to directors to executives.

Informal communication network:

The management has not created a network. This network is not maintained or planned in any way. It is more relaxed and easygoing, and it spreads fast across a department or organization. It is not limited to permissions and a pre-established distribution channel.

1.9.4 Communication Barriers:

Though the communication appears to be simple, it is not so in reality due to the complexities of the people involved and their surroundings. There are some barriers that make communication incomplete, ineffective and imperfect. These barriers are:

- **Physical barriers:** Separate working areas for people of different status
- **Perceptual barriers:** It depends on how our thoughts, assumptions, and perceptions shape our own realities about a person, people, thing, job, etc.
- **Emotional barriers:** The communication should be free and open, it should not be influenced by emotions like fear, mistrust, and suspicion.
- **Cultural barriers:** The people have to work with people of different cultures and behavior. One should adopt the behavioral pattern of the group.
- **Language barriers:** To improve our personality, we need to learn different languages, so as to work with different people in the universal market.
- **Gender barriers:** We have to work in a common platform where men and women are treated equally in the present scenario.
- **Interpersonal barriers:** These are due to less contact with people, rituals, working activities, honesty, etc. leading to maintaining distance from others.

Tips for effective communication/ How to overcome barriers to communication

1. Know the topic - Know what you are talking or writing about.
2. Be focused – communication should be clear, crisp, and to the point.
3. Brevity is the soul of the wit –say what you want to say in brief. In short, simple sentences.
4. Know your audience – know to whom you are talking or writing.
5. Create the right ambiance –create a good atmosphere with proper sound and light.
6. Be positive - relieve stress, and negative feelings and empathize.
7. Use Body language - Use gestures, and facial expressions to convey positive feelings.
8. Learn to listen - listen to what the other person is trying to communicate.
9. Be careful with the usage of words.

10. Maintain eye contact.

1.10 Types of Communication

Communication can be categorized into **three** basic types:

1. Verbal communication- in which you listen to a person to understand their meaning;

- Advantages: Speed and feedback.
- Disadvantage: Distortion of the message.

2. Written communication- in which you read their meaning;

- Advantages: Tangible and verifiable.
- Disadvantages: Time-consuming and lacks feedback.

3. Nonverbal communication- in which you observe a person and infer meaning.

- Advantages: Supports other communications and provides a visual expression of emotions and feelings.
- Disadvantage: Misperception of body language or gestures can influence the receiver's interpretation of the message.

Team Building and Teamwork Skills

- All teams are groups whereas all groups are not teams.
- A **team** is a group of individuals, all working together for a common purpose or goal.

Teamwork: Teamwork is the ability to work together toward a common vision.

Team Building

Team building is the process of turning individuals into team players. Teams have different needs. People should be selected for a team on the basis of their personalities and preferences. People should be matched to the roles they are intended to perform.

1.11 The different aspects of team building are

1. Selection and Training – Select people possessing interpersonal skills. People with good individual accomplishments can be trained to become team players.
2. Allocation of roles and promoting diversity.
3. Establish goals – specific, measurable, and realistic performance goals.
4. Leadership and structure - to provide focus and direction.
5. Evaluation of Performance and Reward System

Skills needed for teamwork

- Besides technical proficiency, you need to have a variety of social skills desired for successful teamwork. They are
- Listening: it is important to listen to others' ideas and plans. That will help to emerge.
- Questioning: It is important to ask questions and discuss the objectives of the team.
- Persuading: It is important to exchange, defend, rethink, and if needed change ideas.
- Respecting: It is essential to respect others' ideas and views when they are worth it.
- Helping: it is a core principle in teamwork.
- Sharing: Sharing creates a conducive environment for the team to work.
- Participating: It makes the work easy and simple.
- Communication: have open communication to work effectively and efficiently in a team.

1.12 Model of Team Building:
In modern practice, there are five stages of team building

1. **Forming**- In this stage, most team members are positive and polite. Members make an effort to get to know their new colleagues. The leader plays a dominant role because team members' roles and responsibilities are not so clear at this stage. Training is the leader's main task.
2. **Storming**- Conflicts emerge during this period as members try to establish themselves. Confusions around goals and roles begin to surface. This is the growth stage of the team. The leader exercises leadership skills. He ensures that team members continue to learn.

3. **Norming-** Gradually members start to resolve their differences, appreciate colleagues' strengths, and respect the authority of the leader. Members develop a stronger commitment to the team goal.

4. **Performing-** High-performing teams reach this stage and achieve the team's goal. The team members are now competent, autonomous, and able to handle the decision-making process without supervision.

5. **Adjourning-** Adjourning, is the breakup of the group, hopefully when the task is completed successfully, its purpose is fulfilled; everyone can move on to new things, feeling good about what's been achieved. Teams are disbanded at this stage. For example, project teams exist for only a fixed period.

1.13 Characteristics of Effective Teams

Some characteristics of effective teams are

1. explicit instructions and obligations.
2. knowledgeable individuals.
3. proper operational processes.
4. healthy interpersonal connections.
5. shared victories and setbacks serve as a motivating force.
6. favorable external connections
7. give inspiration and stimuli.
8. Synergy may take many different forms in teams.
9. always evolving.
10. team members have a sense of specialness.

1.14 Steps to build an effective team

4 Step to
Build an Effective Team

Find the Right People 01

When it comes to building a team, trust is hard to define, but hiring the right people for the task is crucial.

02 ### Orient new members

Leaders set the work scope, set deadlines, describe each member's responsibilities, and monitor performance.

Team communication 03

Communicating goals and responsibilities, as well as motivating the team, is crucial for a leader.

04 ### Support team growth

As team members grow in confidence in their roles, they start to work together more easily.

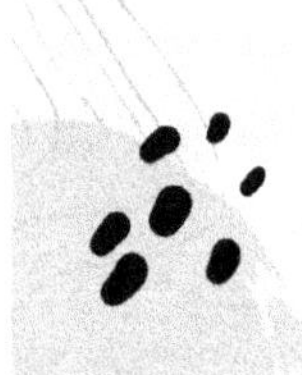

1.15 Role of a Team Leader:

1. Setting objectives for future performance is part of planning.
2. Organizing entails delegating duties to attain a goal.
3. Giving orders to carry out duties is what commanding entails.
4. Coordination entails bringing everyone together to accomplish the same objective.
5. Controlling to track progress toward objectives
6. Respect others' rights, dignity, viewpoints, and talents.
7. Understands democratic ideas.
8. Works with a group to steer them toward a common objective.
9. Understands his or her own talents and shortcomings.
10. Shows self-assurance and a readiness to take a position.
11. Effectively communicates.
12. Demonstrate self-initiative, desire to work, and job completion.
13. Shows optimism, is open-minded, and is willing to compromise.
14. Others are praised and given credit.
15. Dedicated to exceeding expectations.

1.16 Role of Team Members:

Being able to work in a team is important in today's work environment. For a team to function well, a team member has to understand his role and the roles others play. There are many skills involved in effective teamwork.

- listen and share ideas
- Share tasks and responsibilities
- decision-making and problem-solving skills
- resolve any 'differences' and show commitment
- cooperate with others
- encourage each other
- recognize and use each other's strengths
- develop a positive working relationship
- take time to get to know each other
- exhibit flexibility
- remember in a team, 1 + 1 = 3

1.17 Comparison between Team and Group

Group V/s Team

• A group is a set of people, usually from 3 to 20.	• A team is a specialized group with lesser number of people (3-12 people).
• Some degree of interaction and shared objectives among group members.	• Higher degree of coordinated interaction among group members.
• Selection of group is simple and easy.	• Selection is based on skills required.
• Focus is on individual goal.	• Focus is on team goal.
• Individual or solo leader.	• Shared or rotating leadership.
• A group works efficiently for short term projects.	• Teams work efficiently for long term projects.
• Come together to share information	• Come together for discussion, decision making, problem solving and planning.
• Produce individual work products.	• Produce collective work products
• Group members are more independent	• Team members are more interdependent.
• No positive synergy (neutral)	• Positive synergy through coordinated effort.
• Overall level of performance is equal to the sum of individual performances.	• Overall level of performance is greater than the sum of individual performances.

Comparison between Team and Group

1.18 Different between Leader and Boss

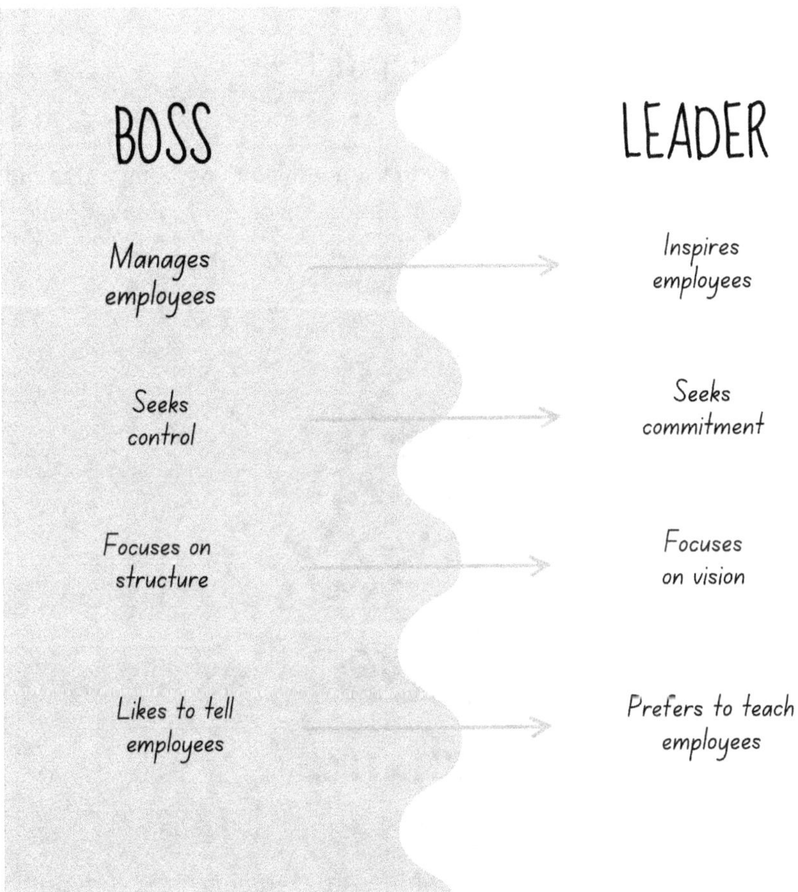

Differences between Leader and Boss

CHAPTER II

Maintenance and TQM

When you maintain a machine, you try to keep it in good working order and address any issues. It is recognized as industrial machinery and equipment maintenance.

Making ensuring that every piece of industrial equipment is constantly operating as effectively as possible is the primary objective of regular maintenance.

It includes standard maintenance such as weekly cleaning, lubrication, and minor adjustments. This enables the early identification and remediation of small problems that may otherwise stop a manufacturing line.

2.1 FUNCTIONS OF MAINTENANCE:

The following are the functions of maintenance in every manufacturing organization:

- Maintenance of the present machinery and apparatus.
- Maintenance of the surroundings and existing buildings.

- Equipment evaluation and lubrication
- Changes to the machinery and buildings that have previously been created.
- Development of new buildings and machinery.
- storing items
- The defense of plants against fire.
- Trash disposal and recycling.
- cleaning solutions
- regulating pollution, noise, etc.
- Records and analyses.
- Preserving spare parts.

2.2 Types of Maintenance

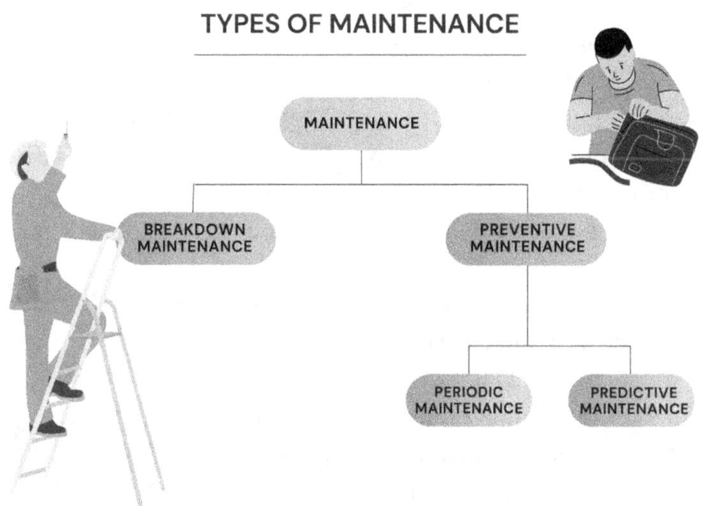

Types of Maintenance

2.2.1 Breakdown maintenance:

- In this type, no care is taken from the machine, until the equipment fails. Then repair is undertaken.
- This type of maintenance is used, when the equipment failure does not affect the operation or production rate.

- Failure of a component of a big machine may be injurious to the operator.

2.2.2 Preventive maintenance:

- It is also known as systematic, planned, or scheduled maintenance.
- Its primary purpose is to identify problem areas and eliminate them before the equipment fails.
- Cleaning, inspecting, lubricating, tightening, and so on are all part of daily maintenance.
- It is feasible to preserve equipment in excellent condition and avoid failure by preventing deterioration.

Periodic maintenance or Time-Based Maintenance (TBM) or Scheduled maintenance

To avoid unexpected failure and process issues, time-based maintenance entails routinely inspecting, maintaining, and cleaning equipment.

Predictive maintenance:

It is a technique used to utilize critical components until they have reached the end of their useful lives by estimating their service life based on inspection or diagnosis.

2.2.3 Advantages of Preventive maintenance

- minimizing productivity loss as a result of equipment malfunction.
- Decreases the cost and time of repairs.
- Efficient utilization of laborers and tools.
- Keep all tools of production in excellent functioning order.
- Reducing accidents and increasing worker safety
- Reduces the overall cost of upkeep.
- Increase output while raising product quality.
- Savings in energy.

2.3 Quality

- The product can please the client.
- The degree of perfection is quality.
- It may also be described as the degree of perfection or the extent to which it satisfies the customer's need.

- It is the capacity to meet the demands and expectations of the client.

"Quality is about meeting the needs and expectations of customers"

- Quality consists of
- adherence to the requirements
- suitable for usage
- Value for money spent
- auxiliary services
- psychological requirements

2.3.1 Functions/Objectives of Quality Control:

- cost reduction
- proper use of the raw resources
- Maintain excellence.
- Ensures client pleasure and reduces complaints from customers.
- Find the problems.
- Lowers the costs for the firm.
- To make anything interchangeable.
- To make something at the best possible price.
- To stop a faulty or broken product from ever reaching the client.

2.4 Advantages /Benefits of Quality Control:

- It aids in sustaining a product's quality, which raises sales.
- The rate of rejection will drop.
- The cost of the inspection is decreased.
- Improves the relationship between a company and its clients, employees, and employers.
- One may get uniformity.
- As a result of the achievement of standardization, production costs will be reduced.

2.5 Factors affecting quality:
Factors affecting quality are

- Men, products, and working conditions
- market analysis
- Money, or the capacity to invest.
- Management standards for quality.
- Methods of production and production designs
- bad packaging
- incorrect mode of transportation
- poor post-purchase support
- Poorly made machinery

2.6 Relation between cost and quality:

- The cost of performing the business quality function is included in the cost of quality.
- It is separated into two groups. Those are

Quality control cost:necessary for achieving high quality

1. Prevention cost
2. Appraisal cost

Quality failure cost: consequences of poor quality.

1. Internal failure cost.
2. External failure cost

Prevention cost:

- These are all of the expenses made in the effort to avoid low quality.
- Costs for planning, documentation, training, process management, etc. Are included.

Appraisal cost:

- It results from the discovery of flaws.
- Measurement, evaluation, or auditing of items, as well as testing and maintenance, are all included.

Internal failure cost:
It is connected to identifying subpar product quality before the product is delivered to the client.

- It involves subpar goods, parts, and material failure, among other things.

External failure cost:

- It is associated with quality problems that occur on the customer side.
- It includes customer complaints, services, replacing and repairing, etc.,

2.7 Total Quality Management (TQM):

- It is the integration of all departments and processes inside a company to accomplish continuous improvement of product and service quality to achieve customer satisfaction.
- It refers to the quality engagement of all employees in a business, including suppliers, distributors, and consumers, in terms of quality satisfaction.
- All actions such as quality planning, quality operation, and systematic assessment are included.

2.7.1 Functions of TQM:

- Development of products per specification based on the needs of customers with economic considerations.

- Interact with customers in product design.
- Testing reliability
- Quality control for incoming products
- Inspection and testing during manufacture.
- Quality audit.
- Training of staff and customers regarding quality.

2.7.2 TQM Elements

The following are TQM elements. They are

- **Quality awareness:** The products manufactured in the organization have to meet the customer requirement where quality awareness is given to the customer.
- **Management attitudes:** Management attitude should be a dedicated commitment to supporting quality programs with the help of employees having job satisfaction.
- **Tools and techniques such as process management:** It is essential to know what the process is and what we expect from the process.
- **Quality system standards:** Installing a system for managing quality enables an organization to meet product or service requirements consistently.

2.8 Tools and Techniques of TQM:

The following are tools and techniques of total quality management (TQM):

1. Flow charts
2. Control charts
3. Histograms
4. Pareto charts
5. Check sheets
6. Scatter diagram and
7. Cause and effect diagram
8. 5 – S
9. Poka-yoke
10. Kaizen
11. Re-engineering
12. Six Sigma

2.9 Flow Chart

The Process Flow Chart provides a visual representation of the steps in a process. It is a tool that will help you visualize organizational processes.

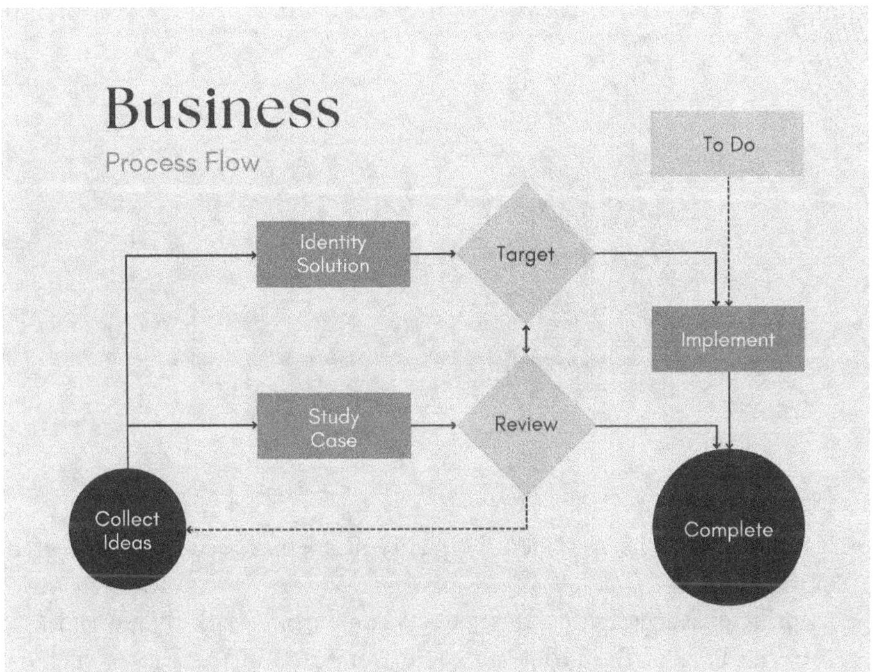

2.9.1 When to use

One of the first activities of a process improvement effort is constructing a flowchart. It provides the following benefits:

1. It gives a clear understanding of the process.
2. Facilitates teamwork and communication.
3. Helps to identify non-value-added operations.

2.9.2 Method:

A flowchart may be built using a variety of symbols, the most popular of which are illustrated below:

Determine the steps of the process and link them with direction arrows. A flowchart has two levels: the micro level, which is a detailed picture of your operations that includes every step and decision, and the macro level, which is a more generalized view of the process. Following that, you must keep track of every step and choice you make during the process.

2.10 Pareto Charts:

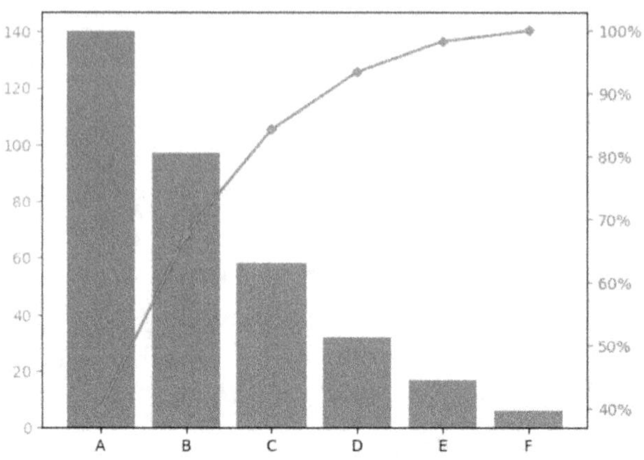

- It is a technique used to identify quality problems based on their degree of importance
- Its principle suggests that most effects come from relatively few causes.
- In terms,80% of the problems come from 20% of the causes such as machines, raw materials, operators, etc.,
- Therefore, efforts are made at the right 20% can solve 80% of the problems.
- Double Pareto charts can be used to compare 'before and after situations.
- It is generally applied to decide where to apply initial effort for maximum effect.

2.11 KAIZEN

- Kai means **change** and Zen**to becomes good**. I.e., Change **To Become Good.**
- It is also known as **continuous improvement.**
- It is a culture of sustained continuous improvement focusing on eliminating waste in all systems and processes of an organization.

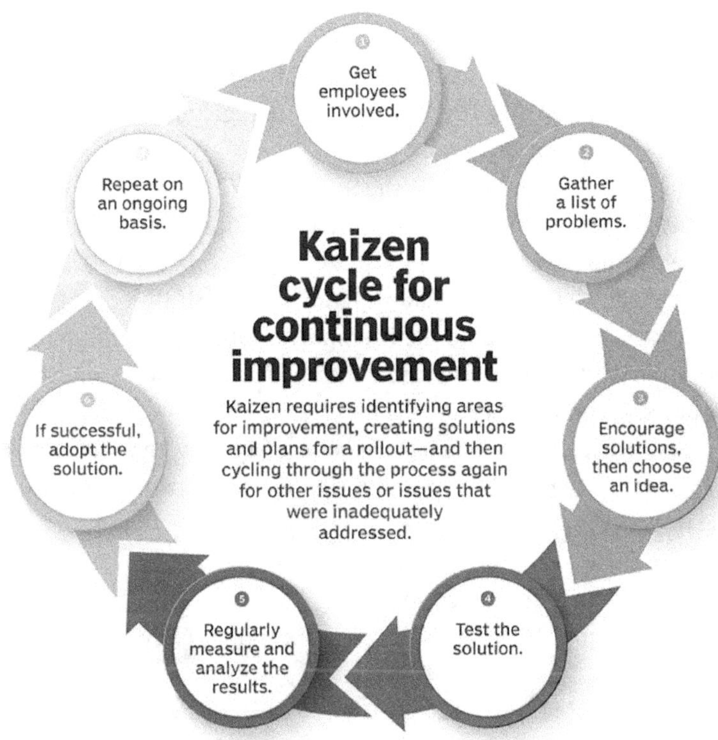

2.11.1 The three key elements of Kaizen are

1. Elimination of waste and inefficiency
2. The 5S framework for good housekeeping
3. Standardization.

2.11.2 Benefits of Kaizen:

1. Realization of immediate results
2. Involvement of the workforce
3. Incorporation of visual action-oriented tasks
4. It is an ongoing exercise, once this concept is learned.
5. This involves creative ideas which cost less to the organization.
6. Employees think from a business perspective.

7. It will facilitate team concepts within the organization.

2.12 Six Sigma :

- It is a Motorola trademark that has been registered and is used as a management tool for quality assurance.
- By identifying and eliminating the sources of mistakes and defects and reducing variability in the production and business processes, it aims to increase the quality of process outputs.
- It is defined as any flow that prevents the fulfillment of customer expectations and requirements. It employs statistical methodologies and builds a particular infrastructure of individuals in the business, such as black belts, green belts, etc.
- It aspires to excellence and has a vision of quality that corresponds to just 3.4 errors per million possibilities for each transaction involving goods or services.

2.12.1 Approaches for six sigma:

There are two approaches to achieving six sigma. They are

1. DMAIC: Define, Measure, Analyze, Improve and Control.
2. DMADV: Define, Measure, Analyze, Design, and Verify.

DEFINE All products by making a list of them along with corresponding results.

MEASURE: Define needs in terms of essential inputs for products/ projects selected.

ANALYZE: Analyze the collected data results and lay the groundwork for improving the process.

IMPROVE: Improve design, performing tasks, implementation, results, etc.,

CONTROL: It reviews the entire process to ensure that the appropriate changes have been made and maintain those changes.

VERIFY: Verify the design, performance, and ability to meet customer needs.

2.12.2 Benefits of six sigma:

- It guarantees improved product quality.

- It makes product delivery predictable.
- It supports increasing productivity.
- Rapid reaction to changing client demands is beneficial.
- It makes it easier to create and release new items into the market.

2.13 Quality Management Service (QMS):

- A quality management system by the ISO 9000 family of certifications encompasses quality management processes, procedures, and skills.
- It helps organizations fulfill quality, regulatory, and customer satisfaction requirements while helping an organization implement future quality improvement initiatives.

ISO 9000:2000 Quality Standards-ISO 9000, ISO 9001 & ISO 9004:

- ISO stands for International Organization for Standardization.
- It is an international body that consists of representatives from more than 90 countries.
- BIS (Bureau of Indian Standards) is the Indian representative of ISO.
- ISO 9000 standards expect firms to have a quality manual that meets ISO guidelines, document
- Quality procedures and job instructions and verification compliance by third-party auditors.

- ISO 9000 series has five international standards on quality management, which are listed below

- ISO 9000:2000
- ISO 9001:2000
- ISO 9002:2000
- ISO 9003:2000
- ISO 9004:2000

The task of Each Standard:
ISO 9000: QMS-Fundamentals and Standards:

i. This provides guidelines for the selection and use of quality management and quality assurance standards.

ISO 9001: QMS-Requirements:

v. It has 20 elements covering design, development, production, installation, and service.
v. This applies to industries that are doing their design and development, production, installation, and service.

ISO 9002:

v. It has 18 elements covering production and installation.
v. It is the same as ISO 9001 without two tasks. Viz., design and development.
v. It is also applicable for the units, excluding R & D functions.

ISO 9003:
It has 12 elements covering final inspection and testing for laboratories and warehouses etc.,
ISO 9004: QMS – Guidelines for performance:

v. This provides guidelines to interpret quality management and quality assurance.

2.13.1 Benefits of ISO 9000 series:

- This offers a commercial edge both locally and internationally.
- Product quality is consistent.
- Clarity is added to the quality system through the documentation of quality processes.
- It guarantees that all organizational members get sufficient, frequency, and high-quality training.
- The consumer benefits of a cost-effective purchasing process.
- Customers that purchase ISO-certified items won't have to spend much on inspection and testing.
- It contributes to increased productivity.
- Procedures and paperwork are involved.

2.14 PROCEDURES AND DOCUMENTS INVOLVED IN ISO 9000 SERIES CERTIFICATION.

Procedures:

- First, national certification is necessary. I.e., in our country, BIS gives a national certification IS: 14000 which is equivalent to ISO: 9000.
- The following steps are involved in registration.

1. Management commitment.
2. Prepare the workmen for change
3. Select the appropriate model like 9001, 9003, etc., which is suitable for the organization.
4. Study the selected model.
5. Arrange the training of leaders and coordinators.
6. Prepare a checklist, analyze the documents and categorize the elements.
7. Prepare the corporate quality manual.
8. Prepare procedure manuals, operational manuals, and work instructions.
9. Update all drawings and specifications.
10. Provide tooling, equipment, facilities, etc., to meet standards.
11. Carry internal audit
12. Take corrective actions.
13. Apply for trial/external audit.
14. Implement the recommendations
15. Application for registration to BIS or any internationally recognized body.

16. After the application is received from the organization, the document quality system will be examined by the certifying agency.
17. If they found it is satisfactory, they will grant a license
18. The certificate awarded is valid for 3 years.
19. During this period, surveillance audits are conducted to ensure that the documented quality system is being effectively maintained. Then the certificate is renewed further if required.
20. Otherwise, the mistakes have to be corrected by the applicant.
21. Documentations move from one level to the next level in the order listed below.

POLICY: Defines what will be done and why it is stated. It is a policy manual.

PROCEDURE: It is quality procedures that describe Who, When, and Where.

PRACTICES: Defines how the job is done.

RECORDS: It is a document that includes policies, procedures, and work instructions to be followed.

CHAPTER III

Energy Management

Energy Management

- Planning and running energy production and consumption units are included in energy management.
- Monitoring, managing, and preserving energy inside an organization is known as energy management.

Importance of Energy Management System

Energy management is essential for preserving energy in your businesses. A few simple cleaning steps might help companies save money on electricity. Because of this, an organization must prioritize energy management.

Cost reduction is the most important component of energy saving. Most businesses may save expenditures by up to 20% by maximizing their energy use.

Reduce risk: Cutting down on energy use helps to lessen the danger of changing energy costs and supply issues.

Reduce carbon emissions: Energy conservation reduces carbon emissions as well as other harmful environmental effects. Create a "Green Image": Cutting carbon emissions helps create a "Green Image."

Energy Conservation

The actions taken to lower energy consumption by using fewer energy services are referred to as energy conservation. This may be done by either utilizing fewer services overall or by using energy more wisely.

Importance of Energy Conservation

The earth provides enough to satisfy every man's needs but not every man's greed said Gandhiji.

Hard facts on why energy conservation is a must are outlined below.

- We use energy faster than it can be produced; the most popular sources, coal, oil, and natural gas, require thousands of years to generate.
- Despite having 16% of the global population, India only has around 1% of the world's energy resources.

- Non-renewable energy sources account for 80% of the fuel we use. According to calculations, our energy supply may only be accessible for another 40 years or more.
- Energy conservation helps the country save a lot of money since imports meet over 75% of our crude oil requirement, which would cost around Rs. 1,50,000 crore per year.
- Saving energy allows us to save money.
- We save energy when we conserve energy. When we use fuel wood efficiently, our demand for it decreases, as does the work necessary to get it.
- Energy generated equals energy saved: two units of energy are produced for every unit of energy saved.
- Save energy to reduce pollution - Energy use and production account for more than 83 percent of greenhouse gas emissions and a considerable proportion of air pollution.

An old Indian saying describes it this way - The earth, water, and the air are not a gift to us from our parents but a loan from our children. Hence we need to make energy conservation a habit.

Strategy/Methodology of Energy Management

Strategies/Methodologies of energy management are listed below

1. Identification of types of equipment/inefficient areas.

    a. Knowledge of the type of energy being used
    b. Study of machines/technology employed
    c. Identification of major energy consumption areas
    d. Process study to identify the inefficient use of energy

2. Identification of technological prerequisites
3. Discussion, brainstorming, and determination of resource requirements
4. Manpower, machine, and technology management
5. Evaluate your activities to calculate the rate of return.
6. Implementation of new processes/technologies/machines
7. Rethink your actions/efforts.

Energy Management Techniques

The following are the essential techniques needed for successful energy management

1. Self-knowledge and awareness among the masses
2. Re-engineering and evaluation
3. Technology upgradation

We use energy more quickly than it can be supplied, even though the most common sources—coal, oil, and natural gas—take thousands of years to create.

India only possesses around 1% of the world's energy resources while having 16% of the global population 80% of the fuel we consume comes from non-renewable energy sources, which make up the majority of the energy we utilize. Projections indicate that our energy source may only be available for another 40 years or more. Saving energy helps the nation save a lot of money since more than 75% of our crude oil demands are fulfilled by imports, which would cost over Rs. 1, 50,000 crores annually.

By utilizing less energy, we can save money. We save energy by doing so. When we utilize it effectively, both our need for fuel wood and the effort required to get it decrease. Energy creation equals energy conservation because two units of energy are produced for everyone that is saved. Conserve energy to cut down on pollution Energy usage and production are responsible for a significant portion of air pollution and more than 83 percent of greenhouse gas emissions.

Energy Crisis

An energy crisis can be defined as " a situation dealing with a definite difference between power supply and demand"

Causes of Energy Crisis

1. Overconsumption puts pressure on fossil fuels like oil, gas, and coal, which in turn may put a burden on our water and oxygen supplies by producing pollution.

2. Overpopulation: Another driver of the issue has been the world's population growth, which has increased demand for fuel and goods.

3. Poor Infrastructure: Another cause of energy scarcity is the aging infrastructure of power generation equipment.

4. Untapped Renewable Energy Options: Renewable energy sources may help lessen our reliance on fossil fuels while simultaneously lowering greenhouse gas emissions.

5. Delay in Power Plant Commissioning: In a few nations, there is a substantial delay in the commissioning of new power plants that may cover the gap between energy demand and supply.

6. Energy wastage: In most areas of the globe, people are unaware of the need of saving energy. It is restricted to books, the internet, newspaper advertisements, lip service, and seminars. Things will not change any time soon until we give it serious consideration.

7. Bad Distribution System: A poor distribution system causes frequent tripping and failure.

8. Major Accidents and Natural Catastrophes: Major accidents, such as pipeline bursts, and natural calamities, such as volcanic eruptions, floods, and earthquakes, may both disrupt the energy supply.

9. Wars and attacks: Wars between nations may also disrupt energy supplies, particularly in Middle Eastern countries such as Saudi Arabia, Iraq, Iran, Kuwait, UAE, and Qatar.

10. Miscellaneous Factors: Tax increases, strikes, military coups, political crises, extremely hot summers, or freezing winters may produce an abrupt spike in energy demand and suffocate supplies. A strike by unions in an oil-producing company may undoubtedly result in an energy catastrophe.

Energy Management Software (EMS)

Energy Management Software (EMS) refers to a variety of energy-related software applications which may provide utility bill tracking, real-time metering, building HVAC and lighting control systems, building simulation and modeling, carbon and sustainability reporting, IT equipment management, demand response, and energy audits.

Energy management software often provides tools for reducing energy costs and consumption for buildings or communities. EMS collects energy data and uses it for three main purposes: Reporting, Monitoring, and Engagement. Reporting may include verification of energy data and setting high-level energy use reduction targets. Monitoring may include tracking energy consumption to identify cost-saving opportunities. Engagement can mean real-time responses (automated or manual between occupants and building managers to promote energy conservation.

Various Stages of Energy Management Software
Data Collection

Data from real-time and historical intervals are gathered by energy management software. Interval meters, Building Automation Systems (BAS), utilities, and sensors on electrical circuits are all used to gather the data. An analysis of previous bills may be utilized to compare energy use before and after the EMS.

The most often tracked utilities are electricity and natural gas, however, some systems also track steam, water consumption, and even locally produced energy. The markets for EMS data collecting have seen accelerated expansion thanks in part to renewable energy sources.

Reporting

Owners and executives that wish to automate energy and emissions audits are the target audience for reporting solutions. When opposed to manual reporting, the program allows for the aggregation or comparison of cost and consumption data from several buildings, saving time. EMS provides more thorough energy data. Prioritizing energy-saving activities may be done using this information.

Metered and billed usage may be compared using bill verification. By comparing electricity demand charges to consumer prices, for instance, bill analysis may also show the effect of various energy costs.

Monitoring

Monitoring software keeps track of and shows historical and real-time data. EMS often incorporates a variety of benchmarking techniques, including weather normalization, energy usage per square foot, and more sophisticated analysis to spot unusual demand. Facility or Energy Managers may find chances for savings by seeing precisely when energy is consumed and by recognizing anomalies. The EMS may be used to find and organize initiatives including demand reduction, equipment replacement, equipment retrofits, and the elimination of unneeded loads. When consumption levels surpass pre-set criteria based on usage or cost, EMS may provide notifications through text or email messages. To identify whether consumption is excessively high or low, these thresholds may either be set at absolute values or calculated using an energy model. More lately, tablets and smartphones have moved into the mainstream as EMS platforms.

Engagement

Engagement may relate to automatic or manual reactions to data on energy that has been gathered and examined. Building control systems can react to energy fluctuations just as quickly as a heating system can in response to changes in temperature. Demand surges may cause equipment to shut down automatically or with human assistance.

Connecting tenant preferences with building energy use is another goal of engagement. Residents may observe the instant results of their activities thanks to the display of real-time usage data. The software may be used to advertise energy-saving programs, provide residents advice, or create a platform for discussion about sustainability programs.

Energy conservation initiatives that are pushed by the public, like those supported by Energy Education, may be very successful in lowering energy costs and use. A 7% decrease in energy use may be achieved only by informing residents of their real-time use.

Energy and Facility Management Software(EFMS)

An enterprise-wide platform for managing technical data about buildings is referred to as "energy and facility management software," which is the result of the union of "energy management software," "computer-assisted facilities management," and "eas" (Energy Accounting Software). As a result, it entails obtaining and processing the information needed to maintain a reasonable degree of interior comfort while using the least amount of energy.

Purpose of EFMS

An EFMS serves a dual purpose:

- **Tactical:** On a day-to-day operational level an EFMS will help improve comfort level while minimizing energy consumption.
- **Strategic:** On a mid-to-long term scope an EFMS will support the development strategy of the organization, which will support managerial decisions such as systems, vendors or processes efficiencies, ratings, critical areas, etc.

Methodology of EFMS

Information Classes

To achieve its purpose an EFMS integrates several informational classes in a common processing environment, mainly:

- Information on energy usage is often handled by an EMS and acquired from online metering devices (such as Energy meters, Gas meters).
- A BMS often stores system data like HVAC system settings, sensor readings, etc.

- Assets Typical data available in a CAFM system includes building dimensions, floor area, and number, the cooling capacity of installed HVAC systems, maintenance records, etc.
- Weather data is often acquired from locally placed sensors or online weather sources.
- Information on occupancy and use, such as the number of hotel rooms occupied or shoppers served in a store, is often seen in ERPs.
- Information about utility bills is often stored in an EAS (Energy Accounting Software).

Processes

The processes performed in an EFMS fall under the categories:

- **Entry Processes** may be *tactical* such as automated synchronization with a BMS or ERP or *ad hoc* such as the manual entry of utility bills data or the upload of a maintenance log.
- **FDD Processes** (*Faults Detection & Diagnosis*) may include sub-processes for setting various thresholds, selecting from a list of rules which ones should be applied to each specific building/installation, and the tactical application of rule sets and threshold values to an FDD scanning process of building-related data.
- **Work Order Processes** include processes for relaying alerts and faults to users and managing the actions they undertake until the issue is resolved.
- **Reporting Processes** that involve the tactical creation of visualization elements and reports or ad hoc querying processes for data mining and faults investigation.

Block Diagram Representation of EFMS

The block diagram representation of EFMS used for energy management of the building is shown below

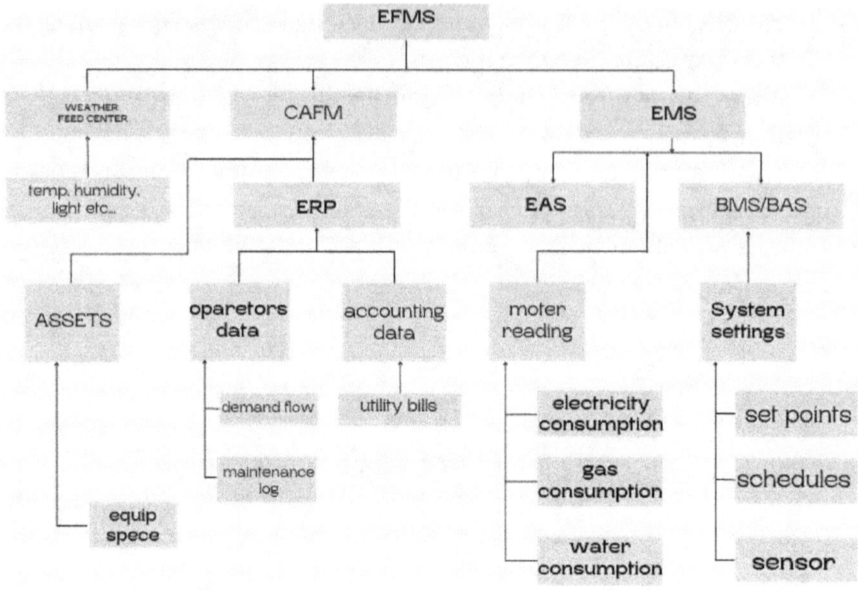

Fig: Block Diagram representation of EFMS

Terminologies

ERP - Enterprise Resource Planning

EMS - Energy Management Software

CAFM - Computer-Aided Facility Management

BMS - Building Management System

BAS - Building Automation System

EAS - Energy Accounting Software

Components

An EFMS should be consisted of at least the following modules:

- **Visualization / Dashboard Module** which will present graphical or table illustrations of energy information (from EMS), system information (from BMS), and Billing information (from EAS).
- **Alarming Module** which will create and manage alarms based on given threshold values and/or Faults Detection & Diagnosis detection methods.
- **Work Order Module** which will create and manage notifications of alarms directed towards appropriate users. The Work Order Module will

manage the actions of users related to each fault along the Fault Cycle (birth, detection, diagnosis, action, evaluation).

- **Data Sources Module** which will manage the connection to and synchronization with the various data sources such as energy management systems and metering devices, BMS, EAS, ERP etc.
- **Reporting Module** which will manage the creation and distribution of energy and facility reports.

Applications of EFMS

Applications of integrated EFMS will benefit most organizations with large and busy facilities, such as

1. Used in malls
2. Applicable in hotels and complexes
3. Used in transportation hubs such as retail chains, restaurants, banks, food store chains, etc
4. Used in commercial property managers to perform an energy audit.

CHAPTER IV

Energy Conservation

Definition

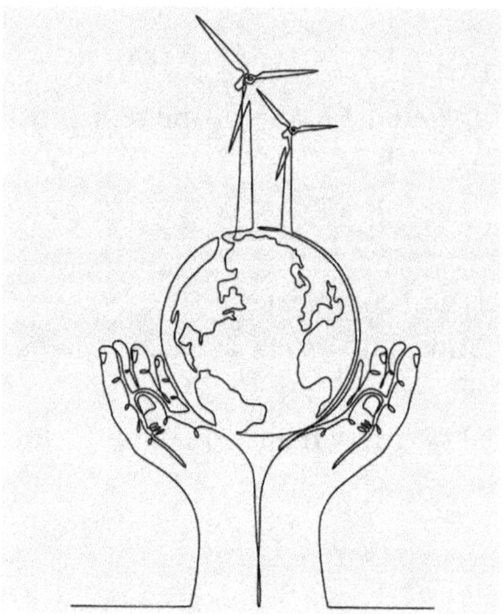

In recent years, India has made tremendous progress toward economic independence. Impressive progress has been made in the fields of manufacturing, agriculture, communication, transportation, and other disciplines that depend on the utilization of energy for growth and economic activity. To achieve the desired increase in GDP, India will need the appropriate input of commercial energy in the form of coal, gas, and electricity. India's fossil fuel supplies are limited and could only last 18 to 26 years. However, the increased ash content of Indian coal may have a substantial influence on greenhouse gas emissions. India, on the other hand, has massive coal reserves that may last for almost 200 years.

The need for energy is always rising, while the cost and availability of energy sources are both rising. Although building a new power plant is costly and takes time, energy-saving programs may swiftly and very cheaply increase the amount of electricity available. Changing the policy's goals from "energy conservation" to "energy efficiency," from "energy inputs" to "effectiveness of energy use," and from "energy services" to "energy services," would be essential. Strategies for demand-side management and end-use energy optimization may allegedly save close to 25,000 MW throughout the whole of India.

Efficiency in energy use and conservation is even more important given that one unit of energy saved at the consumption level reduces the need for new capacity production by two to two and a half times. Furthermore, it is possible to achieve such savings via energy efficiency for less than one-fifth of the cost of constructing new capacity.

4.1 Principles of Energy Conservation

The various principles involved in energy conservation are

1. Optimal control
2. Optimize capacity
3. Optimize load
4. Use efficient processes
5. Reduce losses
6. Energy containment
7. Examine energy conservation opportunities
8. Energy storage facilities

4.2 Need for energy conservation in India

India has advanced quickly toward economic independence in recent years. In the areas of industry, agriculture, communication, transportation, and other disciplines needing the use of energy for development and economic activities, impressive progress has been accomplished. India will need the proper input of commercial energy in the form of coal, gas, and electricity to achieve the planned rise in GDP. Fossil fuel reserves in India are constrained and may only last between 18 and 26 years. India, meanwhile, has enormous coal reserves that might endure for roughly 200 years, albeit the rising ash content of Indian coal could have a significant impact on greenhouse gas emissions.

The need for energy is always increasing, while the available energy sources are getting more expensive and rare. New power production plant construction is expensive and takes time, however, energy-saving initiatives may quickly and at a very cheap cost make more power accessible. It would be necessary to change the policy's objectives from "energy conservation" to "energy efficiency," from "energy inputs" to "effectiveness of energy usage," and from "energy services" to "energy services." End-use energy efficiency and demand-side management strategies may reportedly save close to 25,000 MW throughout all of India.

Given that one unit of energy saved at the consumption level decreases the requirement for new capacity generation by two to two and a half times, efficient energy usage and conservation become even more crucial. Furthermore, achieving such savings via energy efficiency may be done for less than one-fifth the price of adding new capacity.

4.3 Importance of Energy Conservation

The earth provides enough to satisfy every man's needs but not every man's greed said Gandhiji. Hard facts on why energy conservation is a must are outlined below.

- We use energy more quickly than it can be created; the most common sources, coal, oil, and natural gas, take thousands of years to develop.
- India only possesses around 1% of the world's energy resources, although having 16% of the global population.
- 80% of the fuel we consume comes from non-renewable energy sources, which are the majority of the energy sources we utilize. There are estimates that our energy supplies may only be available for another 40 years or so.
- Energy conservation helps the nation save a lot of money since over 75% of our crude oil demands are satisfied by imports, which would cost approximately Rs. 1, 50,000 crores annually.
- Saving energy helps us save money.
- We save energy when we save energy. When we utilize fuel wood effectively, our need for it decreases, as does the effort required to obtain it.
- The energy created equals energy saved: two units of energy are produced for every unit of energy saved.
- Conserve energy to lessen pollution - Energy usage and production account for more than 83 percent of greenhouse gas emissions and a

significant percentage of air pollution.

An old Indian saying describes it this way - The earth, water, and the air are not a gift to us from our parents but a loan from our children. Hence we need to make energy conservation a habit.

4.4 The Energy Conservation Act, 2001 and Its Features

The Government of India has enacted the Energy Conservation Act – 2001 for high energy saving potential and its benefits, reducing the gap between demand and supply, and reducing environmental emissions through energy saving.

4.4.1 Important features of the Energy Conservation Act are:

- **Standards and Labeling** Through the S&L program, customers are guaranteed access to only energy-efficient products. The following are the key clauses of the EC Act on Standards and Labeling: Create performance criteria and a labeling system for alerting appliances and equipment.
- **Designated Consumers** The main provisions of the EC Act on designated consumers are: The government would notify energy-intensive industries and other establishments as designated consumers A list of designated energy consumers are intensive industries, Railways, Port Trust, Transport Sector, Power Stations, Transmission & Distribution Companies, and Commercial buildings or establishments;

4.4.2 Certification of Energy Managers and Accreditation of Energy Auditing Firms

The Act's key objectives in this area are: A Certification and Accreditation program would be used to create a cadre of professionally competent energy managers and auditors with experience in policy research, project management, finance, and the execution of energy efficiency projects.

Energy Conservation Building Codes: The main provisions of the EC Act on Energy Conservation Building Codes are: The BEE would prepare guidelines for Energy Conservation Building Codes (ECBC);

Central Energy Conservation Fund: The EC Act provisions, in this case, are: The fund can be utilized for energy conservation and its promoting activities.

Bureau of Energy Efficiency (BEE): The BEE has set to reduce energy consumption intensity in the Indian Economy.

4.4.3 Role of the Bureau of Energy Efficiency

The role of BEE would be to prepare standards and labels of appliances and equipment, develop a list of designated consumers, specify certification and accreditation procedures, prepare building codes, maintain the Central EC fund and undertake promotional activities in coordination with center and state-level agencies.

4.5 Role of Central and State Governments:

The following role of Central and State Government is envisaged in the Act

- **Central** - to notify rules and regulations of the Act, provide initial financial assistance to BEE and EC funds, and Coordinate with various State Governments for notification, enforcement, penalties, and adjudication.
- **State** - to amend energy conservation building codes to suit the regional and local climatic conditions, to regulate and enforce provisions of the Act and constitute a State Energy Conservation Fund for the promotion of energy efficiency.

4.5.1 Enforcement through Self-Regulation:

E.C. Act would require the inspection of only two items. The certification of energy consumption norms and standards of the production process by the Accredited Energy Auditors.

4.5.2 Penalties and Adjudication:

Penalty for each offense under the Act would be in monetary terms i.e. Rs.10,000 for each offense and Rs.1,000 for each day for continued non Compliance.

4.6 National Institutions Promoting Energy Conservation in India

1. Bureau of Energy Efficiency (BEE)
2. Petroleum Conservation Research Association (PCRA)
3. Indian Renewable Energy Development Agency (IREDA)
4. National Productivity Council (NPC)
5. National Council for Cement and Building Materials (NCB)
6. The Energy Research Institute (TERI- TATA Energy Research Institute)
7. Confederation of Indian Industry (CII)
8. Federation of Indian Chambers of Commerce and Industry (FICCI)

4.7 Role of IREDA in Energy Conservation

The Indian Renewable Energy Development Agency Limited (IREDA), under the Ministry of New and Renewable Energy, is a government of India enterprise (MNRE). In order to promote renewable energy sources including wind, hydro, solar, biomass, waste to energy, etc., the Public Limited Government Company known as IREDA was founded in 1987 as a Non-Banking Financial Institution. Later, it expanded into energy conservation and efficiency. With the slogan "ENERGY FOR EVER," IREDA provides funding for initiatives including renewable energy, energy efficiency, and conservation.

IREDA may provide financial assistance to industries for energy-saving initiatives up to 70 to 75 percent of the total project cost at a long-term, low-interest rate.

4.7.1 Energy conservation in Electricity Transmission & Distribution lines

Power generated in power stations passes through large and complex networks like transformers, overhead lines, cables, and other equipment and reaches the end users. It is fact that the unit of electric energy generated by Power Station does not match the units distributed to the consumers. Some percentage of the units is lost in the distribution network. This difference in the generated and distributed units is known as Transmission and Distribution loss. The T & D losses fall into two categories.

4.8 Technical electrical power losses

Technical losses occur when the energy is dissipated by the equipment and conductors in the distribution lines. The losses depend on the network characteristics and mode of operation. There are two categories of technical power losses; fixed technical losses and variable technical losses.

4.8.1 Fixed technical losses

The fixed losses in the distribution lines account for between a quarter and a third of the total technical losses. These are usually in the form of heat and noise and occur whenever the transformer is energized.

The fixed losses are not influenced by the amount of load current flowing, but rather by

- The leakage current losses
- Open circuit losses
- Corona losses
- Dielectric losses

4.8.2 Variable technical losses

The variable losses are proportional to the square of the load current and account to between 2/3 and ¾ of the technical losses in a distribution system. The variable losses arise due to the line impedance, contact resistance, and joule heating losses.

4.8.3 Causes of technical losses

- Inefficient equipment such as transformers, pumps, electrical machines, and industrial loads.
- Inadequate size of the conductor in the distribution lines
- Long distribution lines
- Load imbalance among the phases
- Low power factor.
- Overloading of lines
- Transformers installed far from the load centers
- Haphazard installation of distribution systems to cope with demands to new areas
- Bad workmanship

4.8.4 Commercial (non-technical) power losses

The non-technical losses also referred to as commercial losses, are those related to unmetered supplies, incorrect billing, untimely billing, wrong tariff, defective meters, and energy thefts.

4. 9 Measures to optimize T & D Losses

Losses in the distribution of electricity cannot be eliminated but can be minimized by proper planning of the distribution systems to ensure that power remains within limits. Some of the ways to reduce losses include;

- Use of proper jointing techniques, and keeping the number of joints to a minimum.
- Regular inspection of the connections, isolators, drop-out fuses, LT switches, transformers, transformer bushing-stem, and other distribution equipment.
- Proper selection of conductor size, as well as the transformer in terms of efficiency, size and location. In particular, it is important to locate the distribution transformers at the load center and if possible keep the number to a minimum.
- Feeding heavy consumers directly from the feeders
- Maintain the network components and replace those that are deteriorating, worn out or faulty.
- Proper load management and load balancing

- Use of electronic meters which are accurate and tamper-proof.
- Improving power factor by adding shunt capacitors.

4.9.1 Non-technical losses can also be lowered in a number of ways, such as:

- The use of modern electronic meters can reduce meter errors.
- Close monitoring of unmetered supplies.
- Punishing meter tampering and illegal connections.

4.9.2 Steps used for energy conservation in industries

- Energy prices have increased at an alarming rate, and interest in environmental responsibility is at an all-time high. Many organizations are looking for ways to conserve energy, reduce carbon emissions, and save on overall utility costs.
- While total energy management is very complex, there are some relatively simple strategies that can reduce your company's energy consumption, lower costs, and advance your conservation goals

1. Lighting:

Increasing lighting efficiency is one of the easiest ways to lower energy bills.

Here are a few tips for optimizing the lighting of your business while reducing your electric costs.

- Replace incandescent lighting with compact fluorescent lighting indoors and outdoors. CFL is almost four times as efficient as incandescent bulbs and lasts about 12 times longer
- For outdoor lights, use a timer or photocell so they turn off automatically during the daylight hours
- For indoor lights, adjust lighting levels to your needs with three-way lamps, dimmer switches for overhead lights, and task lighting
- Use 4-foot fluorescent fixtures with electronic ballasts
- Take advantage of natural light by placing work areas near windows
- Install occupancy sensors, so lights go off automatically in unoccupied rooms

2. Motors

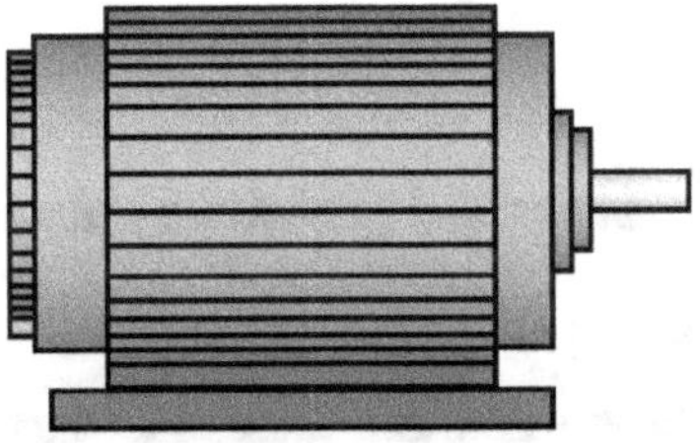

Increasing motor efficiency by replacing inefficient motors with premium energy-efficient motors equates to significant cost savings over the life of the motor. Here are a few suggestions that can help you achieve greater motor efficiency:

- When purchasing a new motor choose the most energy-efficient motors, which may cost about 20 percent more, but can have a relatively short payback to offset these costs.

- Select a lower-power motor and operate it at a higher load factor near optimal efficiency
- Optimize transmission efficiency by using synchronous belts instead of v-belts.
- Consider using a variable-speed drive motor system instead of traditional motors when loads vary significantly over the course of daily use.
- Make sure the voltage of the motor is as close to the design limits, found on the nameplate, as possible.

4. Compressed Air:

Compressed air is produced using electricity, making it a very expensive utility. Compressors are also a major source of energy wastage. Depending on use and pressure, compressed air leaking through a single 3mm hole could cost you around Rs. 4,000 per year. And an idling compressor can still use 40% of its full load. Sopwith off the compressor when not used. Perform regular leak tests on compressed air distribution pipework.

5. HVAC:

Heating, ventilation, and air-conditioning (HVAC) can account for approximately 30% of a business's energy usage. A well-designed system and comprehensive energy-saving techniques can help control your company's utility costs.

6. Refrigeration:

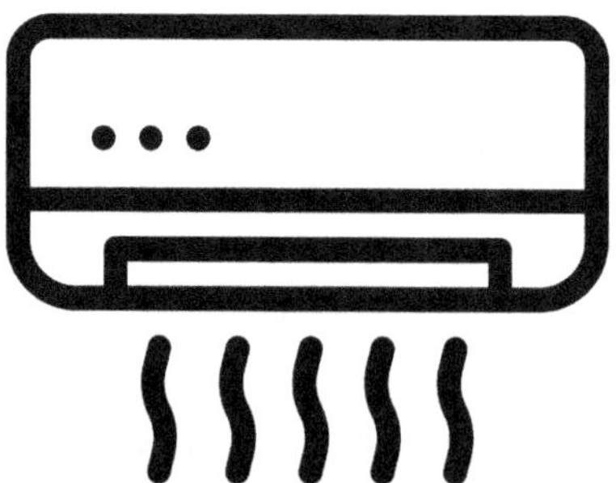

Saving energy on refrigeration can improve your company's profitability while reducing harmful carbon emissions into the environment.

7. Re-cycling.

Recycled aluminum saves 95% of energy and also reduces pollution against virgin aluminum. Using 50% Recycled glass reduces waste by 75% and saves 50% energy. Recycling one glass bottle saves enough energy to light a 100-watt bulb for 4 hours. Pulp and paper making is the 5th largest energy consumer in the world. It also takes 2 to 3.5 tons of trees to make one ton of paper. Recycling of paper saves 65% of energy, uses 80% less water, and reduces 95% of air pollution. Recycling one ton of paper saves 17 trees and 7000 gallons of water.

4.9.3 (5- R to Zero)

4.9.4 Tips for electrical energy conservation in the industrial sector

- **Metering** - Metering can help spot problems and enable them to be resolved.

- **Lighting**-In commercial buildings, lighting accounts for approximately 30% of total energy usage. Savings can be made by deploying efficient lamp technologies, such as LEDs, CFL, and also energy-saving halogen lighting.
- **High-Efficiency Motors / Variable speed drive**- The energy cost to run a motor for two months can be greater than the initial purchase price. Users who employ an effective motor management policy which includes motors, Variable Speed Drives (VSDs), gearboxes, and the driven machine can release further savings.
- **Building Controls**- You can achieve savings of anything up to 30% by installing and maintaining an effective BEMS.

Intelligent Lighting Controls

Implementing intelligent lighting systems such as timers, and occupancy sensors can save over 40% of the energy used in lighting.

Increased Factory or Process Automation

Automation can improve productivity, reduce downtime and minimize maintenance requirements – whilst simultaneously reducing energy consumption.

Power Controls

Power factor correction can improve the usable power available to equipment, and thus maximize its efficiency.

Supply Voltage Optimisation

Optimizing your supply voltage to 225V or 220V can save up to 5-15% in electricity consumption.

Efficient Heating & Cooling Technology

Replacing old and inefficient systems with modern versions can help to save energy.

Combined Heat and Power

Combined Heat and Power (CHP) is the simultaneous generation of usable heat and electrical power in a single process.

4.10 Energy Conservation tips in Domestic Sector

Home lighting

Domestic power consumption in India is about 20% of the total power consumption. Today in India at least 80 percent of the electricity at the household level is wasted because of the kinds of lamps and bulbs we use for lighting our homes. By following simple tips enormous energy can be saved at the household level.

- Turn off lights when not in use
- Clean the dust accumulated on tube lights and bulbs and their fixtures regularly.
- Use ISI-marked electrical appliances and equipment
- Place your tube lights and bulbs in positions where the light is not obstructed.
- Use CFLs and LEDs to save energy. They use less energy as compared to incandescent bulbs and provide the same lighting.
- Use light-colored, loose-weave curtains on windows to maximize daylight inside.
- T5 lights can be used in place of conventional tube lights to save energy.

In Kitchen

- Use energy-efficient stoves.
- Keep the vessels closed with a lid while cooking to reduce cooking time and energy use.
- Soak the food ahead of cooking.
- Dry grinding of food in mixers and grinders takes longer time than wet grinding.
- Microwave ovens consume 50 % less energy than conventional electric/ gas stoves.
- Electric stoves can be turned off several minutes before the specified cooking time.
- Flat-bottomed pans that make full contact with the cooking coil reduce the loss of heat.
- Pressure cookers should be used as much as possible
- Refrigerated items like vegetables, milk, meat, etc should be brought to room temperature before heating/cooking.
- Solar Water Heaters can be used to replace electric water heaters/fuel-based heating systems.

In households electronic devices

- When devices like TV, Computers, and Audio Systems are not in use, the power should be switched off.
- If computers have to be left on, the monitor should be turned off.
- There should be enough space left between a refrigerator and the walls so that air can easily circulate between them.
- Refrigerator door seals should be airtight.
- Avoid putting hot or warm food straight into the refrigerator.
- Washing machines should be used only with full loads.
- Air conditioners having automatic temperature cut-offs should be preferred.
- The ceiling fan should be operated in conjunction with the air conditioner to spread the cooled air more effectively throughout the room. The air conditioner can then be operated at a higher temperature.
- Doors and windows should be sealed properly.

4.11 Tips for energy conservation in Agriculture Sector

The agricultural sector is amongst the major energy-consuming sectors after the industrial sector. The two main energy sources use a substantial amount of High-Speed Diesel and electricity. Electricity consumption in the agriculture sector has been increasing mainly because of greater irrigation needs for new crop varieties and subsidized electricity to this sector.

Tips for Energy Conservation in Agricultural Pump

1. Selection of right capacity of pumps according to the irrigation requirement.
2. Matching of pump set with source of water - canal or well.
3. Matching of motor with appropriate size pump.
4. Proper installation of the pump system - shaft alignment, coupling of motor and pump.
5. Use of efficient transmission system. Maintain right tension and alignment of transmission belts.
6. Use of low friction rigid PVC pipes and foot valves.
7. Avoid use unnecessary bends and throttle valves.
8. Use bends in place of elbows.
9. The suction depth of 6 metres is recommended as optimum for centrifugal pumps. The delivery line should be kept at minimum require height according to requirement.
10. Periodically check pump system and carryout corrective measures - like lubrication, alignment, tuning of engines and replacement of worn-out parts.
11. Over irrigation can harm the crops and waste vital water resource. Irrigate according to established norms for different crop.
12. Use drip irrigation for specific crops like vegetable, fruits, tobacco, etc. Drip systems can conserve upto 80% water and reduce pumping energy requirement.
13. **Service your tube well/pumping station regularly**
14. For diesel-powered irrigation pumps, be sure to match the engine output horsepower with the horsepower demanded by the pump

4.12 Energy Efficiency

"Using less energy to provide the same service" is the definition of energy efficiency. For instance, a compact fluorescent bulb consumes a lot less electrical energy to create the same amount of light as a standard incandescent bulb, making it more efficient.

4.12.1 Significance of Energy Efficiency

You, your nation, and the whole planet gain from energy efficiency, or doing more with less energy. The desire to increase energy efficiency is widespread. Energy consumption reduction lowers energy expenditures. The issue of lowering greenhouse gas emissions is also seen to be solved by using less energy. The International Energy Agency estimates that greater energy efficiency in homes, businesses, and transportation may cut global energy consumption by one-third by 2050 and contribute to the reduction of greenhouse gas emissions.

Because it may be utilized to lower the number of energy imports from other nations, energy efficiency is also considered in many countries as having a positive impact on national security.

4.12.2 Benefits of Energy Efficiency

The benefits of energy efficiency are numerous. But the top five reasons that people, companies and governments choose to use energy more efficiently are:

- Spend less money by using less energy.
- The economy is improved via energy efficiency.
- Environmental benefits come from energy efficiency.
- Efficiency in energy use enhances national security.
- Efficiency in energy use improves the quality of life.

4.12.3 Energy-Efficient Appliances/Devices

Following are the energy-efficient appliances/devices

- Freezers.
- Ovens.
- Stoves.
- Dishwashers.
- laundry machines.
- Dryers.

The above modern energy-efficient devices use significantly less energy than older appliances. Current energy-efficient refrigerators, for example, use 40 percent less energy than conventional models did in 2001.

4.13 Star Rating

The star labels on televisions, computer monitors, refrigerators, air conditioners, dishwashers, washing machines, and dryers, can show a maximum of ten stars. That is, the least efficient models have one star while the most efficient models can have up to ten stars.

4.13.1 Energy-efficient motors

Energy-efficient motors are often more durable than NEMA (National Electrical Manufacturers Association) B motors of the same size and use less power. Efficiency for an electric motor is the proportion of the mechanical power it produces (its output) to the electrical power it receives (input).

A motor that is 85% efficient will thus transform 85% of the electrical energy it receives into mechanical energy. An increase in motor temperature causes the last 15% of electrical energy to be lost as heat. Improved motor designs and premium materials are used in energy-efficient electric motors to lower motor losses and increase motor efficiency. Less heat is lost and less noise is released as a consequence of the enhanced design.

413.2 Applications of Circumstances where energy-efficient motors are used

Energy-efficient motors are considered in the following circumstances

- For all new installations
- When major modifications are made to the existing process
- For all new purchases of equipment packages that contain motors.
- When purchasing spares or replacing failed motors.
- Instead of rewinding old, standard efficiency motors
- Replace oversized and underloaded motor
- As a part of energy management or preventive maintenance
- When rebates or incentives are offered.

4.13.3 Applications of Energy-Efficient Motors

Energy-efficient motors are used in the following sectors

- Agriculture pumps
- Water lifting pumps
- 4 Oil well pumps
- Aeronautic applications
- Refrigeration compressor
- Conveyors
- For all new installations
- For all new purchases
- When major modifications are made to the existing process

- For all new purchases of equipment packages that contain motors.
- When purchasing spares or replacing failed motors.
- Instead of rewinding old, standard efficiency motors
- Replace oversized and underloaded motor
- As a part of energy management or preventive maintenance
- When rebates or incentives are offered.

4.13.4 Advantages of Energy-Efficient Motors

The following are the advantages of Energy Efficient Motors:

- Reducing operating costs
- Fewer heat losses
- Extended winding life span
- Extended lubricating grease service life
- Fewer noise levels than other motors
- Reduced energy cost
- Reduces emissions of CO_2

4.13.5 Steps in the selection of an electric drive

The following important points should be considered while selecting a drive. They are

1. Environment
2. Speed range

3. Duty cycle
4. Heating

- **Environment:** Conditions such as ambient temperature, cooling air supply, and presence of gas, moisture, and dust should be considered when choosing a drive for selecting its enclosures and protective features.
- **Speed range:** The minimum and maximum motor speeds for the application should be considered.
- **Duty cycle:** It is important to know the load pattern in selecting the proper drive.
- **Heating:** Proper ventilation is required to achieve minimum heat loss.

4.13.6 Steps to achieve energy conservation in electric drive

It is necessary to minimize energy consumption at all stages of the manufacturing process including the electric drive, which reduces the production cost and product price in the competitive market.

Energy conservation in the electric drive is achieved by reducing the:

1. Electrical transmission losses
2. Conversion losses in the converter
3. Electric motor loss
4. Mechanical losses in the parts of transmission systems
5. Losses caused by control of material flow

4.13.7 Energy conservation in electric drives can be achieved by the:

1. Use of efficient semi-conductor converters
2. Use of energy-efficient motors
3. Use of variable speed drives
4. Proper matching of motor rating and load
5. Provide good quality supply and maintain a higher power factor

6. Regular and preventive maintenance of motors and coupled equipment

4.14 Energy-efficient lighting

The usage of residential lights has dramatically expanded in recent years. Approximately 25% of all domestic power is used for lights. Electric lighting, therefore, uses a lot of energy. Using energy-efficient lighting fixtures, and lighting controls, and thoughtfully designing a lighting system that makes use of both natural and electric sources may save a significant amount of energy. Based on efficiency (lumens per watt), color, temperature, life and availability, switching, dimming capability, and cost, efficient lighting devices are chosen.

For instance, a lot of T8 and T5 linear fluorescent and CFL are great options for today's buildings since they are effective at conserving energy, have a long lifespan, are widely accessible, and are simple to manage. Energy-efficient lighting has been transformed by CFLs and LEDs.

4.14.1 Various energy-efficient lighting sources

The following are the energy-efficient lighting sources

- T12 Fluorescent lamp
- T8 Fluorescent lamp
- T5 Fluorescent lamp
- Compact fluorescent lamp (CFL)
- Light-emitting diodes (LED)

T12, T8, and T5 series fluorescent lamps are invented in the years 1930, 1980, and 2000 respectively. They are energy-efficient lighting sources and consume less energy than incandescent lamps. They differ in the diameter of the tube. Dia of T12 is $1.5''$, T8 is $1''$ and T5 is $0.625''$.

CFLs are simply miniature versions of full-sized fluorescent tubes. They screw into standard lamp holders and give off light that looks just like the common incandescent bulbs.

LEDs are small, solid light bulbs that are extremely energy efficient. New LED bulbs are grouped in clusters with diffuser lenses which have broadened the applications for LED use in the home

4.14.2 Advantages of using Compact Fluorescent Lights (CFLs)

- The use of CFLs reduces electricity costs as they consume 20% to 33% less electricity than an incandescent bulb
- They do not produce too much heat.
- A CFL bulb gives five times more light than an incandescent bulb
- CFL burning hours are 8 times more than the incandescent bulb.
- Instead of using 60 W bulbs, if you would use 15 W CFL bulbs; you can save at least 45 W electricity consumption per hour. Per month you can save up to 11 units of consumption. You can hence reduce costs. CFL bulbs last for at least 5 to 8 months

4.14.3 Disadvantages of CFL

- **Health issues:** ultraviolet and blue light emitted by such devices cause skin allergies and retinal damage in a smaller contribution.
- **Environmental issues:** since CFL contains a small amount of mercury, it may pollute the air and water.
- **Cost:** Usually costs more than an incandescent bulb

4.14.4 Advantages of LED

1. **Efficiency:** Emits more light per watt.
2. **Color:** Emit light of the desired color without using any color filters
3. **Size:** Very smaller size makes it suitable to fix it on PCBs.
4. **On/off time:** On/off time is in terms of microseconds.
5. **Cycling:** Ideal for the use of frequent on-off cycling.
6. **Dimming:** Can easily be dimmed either by reducing forward current or by PWM.
7. **Cool light:** Radiate very little heat in the form of IR
8. **Slow failure:** Failure time is lesser than incandescent bulbs.

9. **Lifetime:** Its lifetime is approximately 35000 to 50000 hours.
10. **Shock resistance:** Being a solid-state component, it is difficult to damage by external shock.
11. **Focus:** Its light can be focused without using external reflectors.
12. **Low toxicity:** It does not contain mercury.

4.14.5 Disadvantages of LED

1. High initial cost
2. Temperature dependence
3. Voltage sensitivity
4. Light quality
5. Area light source
6. Blue hazard
7. Energy-efficient lighting and controls to reduce blue pollution

Apart from FL, CFL, and LED-based lighting systems, many other equipment and control techniques are available to improve the energy efficiency in lighting systems in homes and other commercial applications. Some of these are as follows

- **Electronic ballast:** It acts as a stabilizer.
- **Occupancy sensors:** Occupancy-linked control can be achieved through IR rays, acoustic, ultrasonic, or microwave sensors, which detect either movement or noise in a room. Time-based
- **control: Time-based turn-on**/off switches are low-cost automatic lighting control systems.Daylight
- **linked control:** Photocells or thermistors can be used either to switch on/off ordering.
- **Localized switching:** It is used in large areas. Local switches give individual occupants control. It is possible to switch off artificial lighting in specific areas but still operated in other areas where it is required.

415 Power quality

"Power quality is the set of electrical properties that allows electrical system or equipment to function in their desired manner without loss of performance or life". Without the proper power, an electrical device (or load) may malfunction, fail permanently or not operate at all.

Power quality parameters

Power quality is the quality of the voltage rather than power or current. The quality of electrical power may be described as a set of values of parameters, such as:

- Continuity of service
- Variation in voltage magnitude
- Transient voltages and currents
- Harmonics content in the waveforms

4.15.1 Power quality measurable quantities

The main definitions of power quality measurable quantities or occurrence are as follows

1. **Voltage dip:** It is a reduction in the RMS voltage in the range of 0.1 to 0.9 p.u for a duration greater than half a cycle and less than a minute. Oftennis referred to as a 'sag".
2. **Voltage swell:** It is an increase in the RMS voltage in the range of 1.1 to 1.8 p.u for a duration greater than half a cycle and less than a minute. Caused by system faults, load switches,s and capacitor switching.
3. **Transient:** It is an undesirable momentary deviation of the supply voltage or current.
4. **Harmonics:** Harmonics are periodic sinusoidal distortions of supply voltage or load current caused by non-linear loads.
5. **Distorted voltage:** Distorted voltage or current waveforms containing periodic distortions of a sinusoidal nature.
6. **Flicker:** Flicker is a term used to describe the visual effect of small voltage variations on electrical lighting equipment, which are detectable by the human eye is 1-30 Hz.
7. **Voltage imbalance:** Voltage imbalance is defined as a deviation in the magnitude or phase.

8. **Frequency deviation:** It is a deviation in frequency from the normal supply frequency above or below a predetermined level of ±0.1 %.

9. **Transient interruption:** It is a reduction in the supply voltage overloaded current to a level less than 0.1 p.u for a time of not more than 1 minute.

10. **Outage:** It is an interruption that has a duration lasting more than one minute.

4.15.2 Power quality problems and remedies

Power quality-related problems are of most concern, as the wide use of electronic equipment led to a complete change in electrical loads' nature. These loads are the major causes and victims of power quality problems. All these loads cause disturbances in the voltage waveform.

This implies that some measures or remedies are provided by modern electrical networks, to achieve the level of power quality. Power quality problems may take place at different levels such as transmission, distribution,n, and end-usee equipment.

4.15.3 Most common power quality problems

1. Voltage sag or dip
2. Very short interruptions
3. Long interruptions
4. Voltage spikes
5. Voltage swell
6. Harmonic distortion
7. Voltage fluctuations
8. Noise
9. Voltageunbalancee

4.15.4 Sources of power quality problems

a. Power electronic devices

b. IT and office equipment
c. Arcing devices
d. Load switching
e. Large motor starting
f. Embedded generation
g. Environmental related damages

4.15.5 *Remedies of power quality problems*

To avoid or reduce power quality problems, the following remedies are taken into consideration.

1. **Good earthing practice: A large** number of power quality problems are caused by improper earthing. Checking earthing regularly in a power quality investigation is important.
2. **Use of U.P.S:** When main disturbances is leading to a reduction in the supply mains voltage below some predetermined level, the U.P.S will help to avoid the causes. Standby UPS, online UP, S, and Hybrid UPS are used.
3. **Local or Embedded Generation:** A form of embedded generation such as microturbines, fuel cells, and Stirling engines are likely to have increased domestic usage and also to provide ride-through for power quality disturbances.
4. **Transfer switches:** These are used to transfer a load connection from one supply to another.
5. **Active filters:** This can be used to control reactive power by the use of inductors and capacitors.
6. **Passive filters:** These are fitted to equipment to remove higher-order harmonic frequencies from the supply.
7. **Static breakers:** Static breakers will allow the isolation of faulted circuits in the shortest time.
8. **Energy storage system:** Energy storage systems have the same basic components, interface with the power system, power conditioning system, charge/discharge control,1 and the energy storage medium itself.

4.15.6 Importance of power factor improvement in energy conservation

Improving the PF can maximize current-carrying capacity, improve voltage to equipment, reduce power losses, and lower electric bills. PF correction capacitors act as reactive current generators. They help offset the non-working power used by inductive loads, thereby improving the power factor.

Power factor can be defined as the ratio of true power to apparent power. True power is the actual power consumed by an electric circuit. Apparent power is the product of the voltage and current of the circuit. In an electrical power system, a load with low p.f draws more current than a load with high p.f for the same amount of useful power transferred. The higher current increases the energy lost in the distribution system. A low p.f is expensive and inefficient and some supply companies may charge additional fees when the p.f is less than 0.95

4.15.7 The low p.f can be improved by using the following devices

- Static capacitors
- Synchronouscondenserr
- Phase advancer

4.15.8 Advantages of Power factor improvement and Correction:

Following are the merits and benefits of improved power factors;

- Increase in efficiency of system and devices
- Low Voltage Drop
- 1Reduction in size of a conductor and cable which reduces the cost of the Cooper
- An Increase in available power
- Line Losses (Copper Losses) I2R is reduced
- Appropriate Size of Electrical Machines (Transformer, Generator,s, etc)

- Remove the Electric Supply Company's low power factor penalty
- Low kWh (Kilo Watt per hour)
- Saving the power bill
- Better usage of power system, lines, generators,s, etc
- Saving in energy as well as rating and the cost of the electrical devices and equipment is reduced

4.16 Pricing of Electricity

Electricity pricing is referred to as electricity tariff or the cost of electricity. It varies largely from country to country, state to state.

4.16.1 Factors influencing the electricity price

In addition to the basic production cost of electricity, electricity prices are set by supply and demand. The following factors also affect electricity pricing.

1. **Fuel prices:** The fuel used to generate electricity in power plants share the primary cost incurred by electrical generation companies.
2. **Hydropower availability:** Snowpack, stream flows, seasonality, salmon, n, etc. All affect the amount of water that can flow through a dam at any given time.
3. **Power plant and transmission outages:** Whether planned or unplanned, outages affect the total amount of power that is available to the grid.Weather-driven
4. **demand:** Electricity demand is driven largely by temperature. Heating demand in the winter and cooling demand in summer.
5. **Economic health:** During times of economic hardship, many factories will cut back their production due to a reduction in consumer demand and therefore reduce production-related electrical demand.

CHAPTER V

Energy Audit

5.1 Energy Audit

An energy audit is an inspection, survey, and analysis of energy flows, for energy conservation in a building, process, or system to reduce the amount of energy input into the system without negatively affecting the output(s).

5.2 Need for Energy Audit

The audit is required to identify the most efficient and cost-effective EnergyConservation Opportunities (ECOs) or Measures (ECMs). An energy audit helps improve the efficient use of available resources. In any manufacturing industry, there are some major operating expenses i.e., material, labor, and energy. Energy is the main component of the cost structure of any product or process.

5.3 An energy audit helps:

- To understand which type of fuel/energy is being used for the process.
- In identifying the quantity and cost of various energy forms.
- In identifying the energy consumption at various levels.
- In highlighting the wastage of energy at various stages.

Improving efficient utilization of available energy resources, it reduces the overall cost of the process, in turn, it reduces the cost of the product.

5.4 Scope of Energy Audit

Energy audit includes

1. Monitoring energy consumption
2. Considering the possibility of savings
3. Recommending appropriate policies for reducing energy consumption
4. Possibility of avoiding losses
5. Detailed analysis of present consumption and past trends
6. Reviewing lighting requirements
7. Check capacities and efficiencies of equipment's
8. Compare standard consumption to actual
9. Need for publicity campaigns

10. Examine the need for automatic controls

5.5 Types of energy audit
There are three types of energy audits:

1. Preliminary Audit or Walk-Through Audit (WTA)
2. General Audit Mini Audit or Energy Diagnosis
3. Investment Grade Audit or Comprehensive Audit

- **<u>Preliminary Audit or Walk-Through Audit (WTA)</u>**: As the name suggests, this audit consists of a walk-through inspection of a facility to identify maintenance, operational or deficient equipment issues and also to identify areas that need further evaluation.
  The results of a Walk-Through Audit include the identification of energy-saving opportunities, a qualitative analysis of the implementation of energy-saving measures, and an estimation of its potential energy-saving.
- **<u>General Audit or Mini Audit or Energy Diagnosis</u>**: This audit includes performing economic calculations and may include using some metering devices to identify actual energy consumption and losses. The results of an Energy Diagnosis include financial analysis for each of the identified measures to categorize and prioritize the implementation of these measures.
- **<u>Investment Grade Audit (IGA) or Comprehensive Audit</u>**: This audit is a detailed account of energy use, including a quantitative study of the implementation with detailed investments and operational and maintenance costs and an analysis of the investment model.

5.6 Methodology of Energy Audit
The methodology, related to the energy audits, can collect and calculate the consumptions measured the calculated theoretical consumptions and the saving measures proposed for each of them. Methodology mainly includes two types

1. Preliminary energy audit methodology
2. Detailed energy audit methodology

Each type of Energy audit methodology includes various phases and steps.

5.7 Ten Steps Methodology For Detailed Energy Audit

Basically, Energy audit is divided into three phases. They are

A. Phase: I cover steps 1 & 2
B. Phase: II covers steps 3 to 9
C. Phase III covers step 10.

Sl.No	Action Plan
1	**PHASE:1** a. Plan & organize visit b. Walk through audit of the set up c. Informal interview with production or plant manager or in charge.
2	Conduct brief meeting / awareness program on energy audit with all divisional heads and persons concerned.
3	**PHASE:II** Primary data collection, process flow diagram, energy utility diagram and collection of any other relevant data's.
4	Conduct survey and monitoring
5	Conduct detailed trials / experiments for the selected energy guzzlers
6	Analysis of energy use
7	Identification and development of energy conservation opportunities
8	Cost benefit analysis
9	Reporting & presentation to top management on findings
10	**PHASE:III** Implementation, commissioning and follow up

5.8 Demand Side Management

Energy demand management, also known as demand-side management (DSM) or demand-side response (DSR), is the modification of consumer demand for energy through various methods such as financial incentives and behavioral change through education.

Demand-side management aims to encourage the consumer to use less energy during peak hours, or to move the time of energy use to off-peak times such as nighttime and weekends.

DSR is a term used for programs designed to encourage consumers to make short-term reductions in energy demand.

5.9 Benefits of DSM

Following are the benefits of the DSM

1. DSM offers the consumer to save on their electricity bill.

2. DSM reduces the use of electricity through various awareness programs.
3. DSM promotes more efficient lighting technology.
4. DSM promotes energy awareness and education
5. Encourage the consumer to use less energy during peak hours and encourage them to use in off-peak hours.
6. It reduces peak consumption.
7. DSM allows the consumer to target price spikes by scheduling power-intensive processes.
8. Improved service to the customer.
9. Reduce pollution
10. Reduce energy cost and improves the economy
11. Less capacity generation and transmission required
12. Low cost of service i.e., maintenance.

5.10 DSM 5 steps in planning and implementation

DSM programs are utility and customer-specific. The various steps involved in implementing a DSM program are as follows.

Step-1: Load research

Step 2: Define load shape objective

Step 3: Asses the program implementation strategy

Step-4: Implementation

Step-5: Monitoring and evaluation

Step-1: Load research

This step assesses the customer base, and tariff load profile on an hourly basis and will identify the sectors contributing to the load shape.

Step 2: Define load shape objective

DSM engineers will define the load shape objectives for the current situation. The various load shape objectives are.

- Peak clipping (reduction in peak demand)
- Valley filling (increased demand in off-peak)
- Load shifting (demand shifting to non-peak period)
- Load building (increased demand)
- Conservation (reduction of utility loads)

Step 3: Asses the program implementation strategy

This step will identify the end-user applications that can be potentially targeted to reduce peak demand.

Step-4: Implementation

This stage will design the program for specific end-use applications such as advertising bills and inserts and focused group meetings as in the case of the industrial sector.

Step-5: Monitoring and evaluation

This step will track the program design and implementation and will compare the same with the proposed goal set by the utility.

5.11 DSM Implementation Strategy

After the analysis, data collected, technologies selected, and program designed, the success of a DSM program can deliver the program to the customers. The acceptance depends on how well the program is carried out.

Implementation is integrally linked to the program design. A poor design may be difficult to implement. Similarly, a good program design is likely to be easier to implement and process to flow smoothly.

However, the best program design is likely to require some adjustment, once the program is implemented. Program designers can rarely think of everything the first time around. A variety of delivery mechanisms is available to assist in the implementation of utility programs. They include:

- In-house staff
- Staff hired temporarily to perform program task
- Market intermediaries (retailers, wholesalers, contractors, engineers etc.)
- Community groups
- Outside consultants skilled in program implementation
- Government agencies

CHAPTER VI

SAFETY AND ENVIRONMENTAL ISSUES

SAFETY:

- The government of India established it in 1912 to guarantee industry safety.
- It is described as a state of being relatively devoid of risk, danger, injury, or the threat of harm or loss to persons and/or property.
- It is used to protect against danger and hazards.

NEED FOR SAFETY:

- An industrial accident happens, leaving the workers temporarily or permanently disabled or dead.
- It includes large losses due to lost man-hours, machine-hours, compensation amount, training for replacement staff members, etc.

- As a result, the requirement for effective safety measures and health programmes can reduce direct and indirect expenses while raising corporate profit.
- To stop accidents, the government has passed rules governing industry safety.

ADVANTAGES OF SAFETY MEASURES IN INDUSTRY:

- increasing the rate of production
- lowering the cost of production
- minimising the equipment and machinery damage
- Accident avoidance
- increases the company's profit by increasing its turnover.

ACCIDENT:

- It may be characterised as an unforeseen incident or a sudden mishap that results in the temporary or permanent disablement of personnel and causes significant financial loss due to unused machine and human resources as well as lost wages, training, and other costs.
- It is often described as any circumstance that obstructs the ordered flow of events.
- It is often described as an unanticipated, unplanned, uncontrolled, and unexpected accident or incident that might harm personnel and equipment, result in fatalities, and impair productivity.

LOSSES DUE TO ACCIDENT:

There are two types of losses takes place in industry. They are

1. Direct losses
2. Indirect losses

1. Direct losses:

- It involves the Compensation insurance, it includes payment and overhead costs.
- Uncompensated wage losses of the injured employee
- Cost of medical care and hospitalization.

2. **Indirect losses:**

It involves

- Loss of time to the injured person
- Loss of time of his fellow workers, who stop work at the time of the accident to help him or to show sympathy.
- Loss of time of supervisor in

a. Assisting the injured worker.
b. In investigation and preparing a report of accident.
c. In making an alternative management.
d. In selecting and training the new worker.

- Loss due to damages caused to the machines.
- Loss due to reduction in efficiency of the worker, when he returns after recovery.
- Loss due to reduction in efficiency of the other workers due to fall in their moral.
- Losses to the injured worker ,in

a. Loss to his income
b. Loss due to medical expenditure
c. Pain felt by the worker, which cannot be compensated /measured.

- Cost of wages paid for time lost by workers not injured.

TYPES OF ACCIDENTS:

1. No injury accidents
2. Trivial of lesser importance
3. Minor accidents
4. Serious accidents
5. Fatal accidents

CAUSES OF ACCIDENTS:

The accidents may be due to:

1. **Technical causes:**

- Electrical and Mechanical factors
- Environmental factors

1. **Human causes (Personal factors):**
2. **Technical causes due to deficiencies:**

Electrical and Mechanical factors.

- Unsafe mechanical design
- Hazardous arrangement – unguarded moving parts
- Poor electrical fittings
- Unsafe workplace
- Improper material handling system
- Defective devices
- Leakage of gas or oil
- Improper maintenance

Environmental factors:

- Too low temperature in work places
- Too high temperature in work places
- High speed of work due to heavy load
- Noise, bad smell and poor house keeping
- Restless work
- Improper ventilation etc.,

Human causes (Personal factors):

- Age and fatigue(Tiredness)
- Health
- Home environment.
- Financial positions
- Lack of knowledge and skill
- Improper attitude towards work
- Mental worriers
- Improper use of machine and tool etc.,
- Delay in decision making in implementation of safety measures.
- Lack of management interest against the safety

Technical causes due to deficiencies:

- Technical causes are due to deficiencies in plant, equipment, tools, material handling system etc.,

ACCIDENT PREVENTIVE MEASURES:
Accident prevention is very essential in an industry in order to reduce operating and production costs and to have the good employee and employer relations. The following are the preventive measures. They are

1. Safe work place layout and working conditions.
2. Safe material handling equipment's are to be used.
3. Personal protective devices have to be used
4. Safety activities in the organization.

1. Safe work place layout and working conditions:

- Every employee has enough space to move and operate
- Good ventilation should be at work place
- Sufficient lighting and shock proof working places
- Should not be any fire hazards
- Air temperature, velocity and purity should be maintained.
- Noise proof working conditions should be there.
- Fencing dangerous work spot.

2. Safe material handling equipment's are to be used:

- Properly maintained lifting machines, chains, ropes or lifting tackles should be used.
- Every hoists and lifts shall be of good construction and adequate strength.
- Every hoist way and lift way shall be sufficiently protected
- Conveyers should be of sufficient strength and trolleys should be compact.

3. Personal protective devices have to be used:

- Protection of head by *safety hard hats.*

- Protection of face by *face mask shields and helmets.*
- Protection of eyes by *using spectacles*
- Protection of other body parts by gloves, aprons, safety shoes, ear plugs, glasses etc.,

4. Safety activities in the organization:

- The new entrants, workers trained in the correct procedure of work
- They are made aware in advance of the danger involved
- Giving training about safety act and safety measures.

ROLE OF SAFETY IN INDUSTRIES

In order to avoid accidents in industries, Government has created factory safety acts. As per these acts the industries have to provide appropriate safety measures to the industry, employees and to the work place. The safety in industries helps in:

1. Increasing the production rate
2. Reducing the production cost
3. Reducing the damage to the machineries, equipment's and workers
4. Preventing accidents
5. Increasing the turnover and hence the profit of the company

SAFETY COMMITTEE

The safety committee's main goal is to increase safety awareness and lessen the possibility of harm or loss. The safety director serves as the committee's chair, and both management and employee representatives are present. The committee is represented by a management, a safety engineer, a doctor, a supervisor, and union officials. The workers are given a collective explanation of safety procedures by all the delegates.The factory will get instructions on safety from the safety committee on a regular basis, as well as training as needed.The committee posts safety banners with recommendations and guidelines for each employee to follow at work. The committee will set up a video film screening regarding workplace safety at the end of each month.

GENERAL FUNCTIONS OF THE SAFETY COMMITTEE

1. Identifying the workplace hazards

2. Enforcement of safety rules
3. Measuring the safety performance
4. Reducing the industrial accidents
5. Creating safety policies
6. Developing and monitoring safety programs

ROLE OF SAFETY COMMITTEE

- inspecting industrial workplaces
- reviewing danger reports from employees
- support for safety training
- Developing the incentive packages for safety
- the creation of a safety newsletter
- putting safety warnings and messages on the train
- Finding jobs that are light duty

SAFETY PROVISIONS UNDER INDIAN FACTORY ACT:
The term "safety provisions" refers to security controls on tools, machinery, or other methods that guarantee security. Under the Indian Factory Act, the following safety measures are included.

- Flywheels, waterwheels, and other spinning components must be fenced off and guarded.
- It is not advisable to overload lifting equipment, such as cranes, pulley block rings or hooks, etc.
- Cleaning, lubricating, or adjusting operating machinery is not permitted to be done by women, children, or unskilled workers.
- A belt drive should be capable of shifting with the right mechanism.
- There should be a suitable layout, suitable ventilation, and adequate lighting.
- It is important to supply enough firefighting tools, appropriate warning signs, and suitable explosive stirring.
- Provide enough pathways, emergency exits, and first aid facilities across the various stores.
- Young people shouldn't be permitted to operate hazardous machinery.
- putting on frequent safety awareness campaigns that highlight appropriate behaviour and guidelines.
- Through training, workers should become more safety-conscious.

- When not in use, the driving belt shouldn't be permitted to lie on the rotating shaft.
- The proper hitting equipment or another effective mechanical device must be offered and indicated.
- Providing a footing and handhold for someone working more than two metres from the ground.
- Self-acting machines' traversing parts shouldn't be permitted to operate on their outward or inward transverse inside 18 inches of any permanent structure.
- All powered equipment that is put in factories must be contained or otherwise properly protected.
- Every hoist and lift must have a decent mechanical design, solid structure, and sufficient strength.
- Lifting tools such as chains, ropes, and tackles must be free from flaws and have acceptable mechanical design, sound materials, and enough strength.
- a sign showing the maximum safe operating speed that is permanently installed close to each rotating equipment.
- Effective precautions must be taken to ensure that the safe working temperature is not exceeded if any operation is conducted at a pressure higher than atmospheric pressure.
- It is necessary to keep all floors, stairwells, steps, passageways, and gangways clear of impediments and slip-rings.
- Every tank, pit, sump, fixed vessel, aperture in the ground or in a floor, or sump that is fixed must be covered or fenced.
- Adult males, adult women, adolescents, and children should not lift or carry more weight than what the state government has set as the maximum.
- In order to safeguard the workers, factories should offer sturdy screens or goggles.
- Any chamber, tank, pit, conduit, or other confined location where it is anticipated that toxic vapours or gases would be present must not be entered or allowed to be entered.
- There is no usage allowed for combustible gas or portable electrical lights.
- Explosions must be avoided by taking reasonable precautions.
- Making provisions for fire escape is necessary.

Ozone Layer

"A stratospheric layer at a height of about 10 km (6.2 miles) that has a high concentration of ozone (O3), which absorbs the majority of the UV light from the sun that is directed toward the earth." The French physicists Charles Fabry and Henri Buisson made the discovery of the ozone layer in 1913. The majority of the ultraviolet (UV) radiation from the Sun is absorbed by the ozone layer, also known as the ozone shield, which is an area of the Earth's stratosphere. Ozone is present in significant amounts (O3). The ozone layer is mostly located in the lower stratosphere, between 20 and 30 kilometers (12 and 19 miles) above Earth, however its thickness fluctuates seasonally and geographically.

Causes of ozone layer depletion

The ozone layer is being depleted as the ozone reacts with chlorine, water vapours and nitrogen oxide released by:

- High altitude aircrafts
- CFC's which are widely used as aerosol spray propellants, refrigerants, fire extiguishers etc.
- Notrogen oxide produced by the action of bacteria in soil
- Large buidup gase and chemicals emitted by industrial plants and automobiles.

Ozone layer depletion process

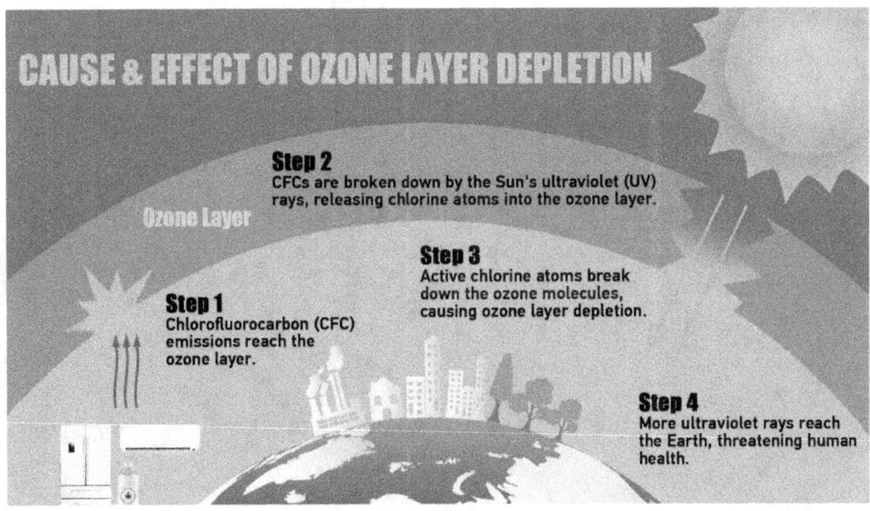

Under certain conditions found in the stratosphere, chlorine is capable of attacking ozone and converting oxygen. A single chlorine molecule can break many thousands of ozone molecules. If the rate of production of chlorofluorocarbons (CFC's) remains constant, the rate of ozone decomposition will increase due to the accumulation of chlorine in the stratosphere, leading to further depletion of the ozone layer. When they reach the stratosphere, they are finally broken down by the sun's UV radiation. This leads them to emit free chlorine. Chlorine combines with ozone, resulting in the chemical process of eliminating ozone molecules known as ozone depletion.

Effects of Ozone Depletion

Human health is adversely affected and crop yields are significantly reduced if the ozone concentration increases near the earth's surface.

Following are the some of the ill effects of ozone depletion:

1. Earth excessive exposure to UV radiation is linked to several health problems in human including eye cataract, skin cancers.
2. Damage to immune system (reduced resistance to diseases).
3. Shorter life of paints and plastics due to deterioration
4. Restricted growth and crop damage.
5. Destruction of aquatic life.

Thus eye concentration of ozone is harmful at lower levels of atmosphere, whereas at higher levels the atmosphere protects us from the UV radiations of the sun.

Global Warming

"A gradual increase in the overall temperature of the earth's atmosphere generally attributed to the greenhouse effect caused by increased levels of carbon dioxide, CFCs(Chlorofluorocarbons), and other pollutants". It is also referred as climate change.

Effects of global warming

Every year, scientists learn more about the effects of global warming, and many believe that environmental, economic, and health implications are expected if present trends continue. Some of the impacts include:

- Earth's temperature will rise by 40 to 60 degrees.
- abrupt shift in the weather.
- Wildfire danger will rise as a result of early snowmelt, severe droughts, melting glaciers, and increasingly acute water shortages.
- Human dwellings suffer damage from rising sea levels.
- Cities, farms, and forests will see more bothersome bugs, heat waves, torrential downpours, and flooding. Agriculture and fisheries will be harmed or destroyed by all those elements.
- Many plant and animal species may become extinct if environments like coral reefs and Alpine meadows are damaged.
- Asthma, allergies, and infectious diseases are all related to rising air pollution.

Environmental Impact Assessment (EIA)

An environmental impact assessment (EIA) is a procedure for determining the anticipated effects of a project or development on the environment while taking into account associated socio-economic, cultural, and human health effects, both positive and negative.

A project's environmental, social, and economic implications may be determined using an EIA tool before a decision is made. It tries to anticipate environmental effects during the planning and design stages of projects, identify strategies for minimising negative effects, adapt projects to the local environment, and give forecasts and choices to decision-makers.

Need of Environmental Impact Assessment

1. Predict the environmental impacts of projects
2. Find ways and means to reduce adverse impacts
3. Shape projects to suit the local environmental
4. Present the predictions and options to the decision makers
5. Waste minimizing, reuse, recycling, disposal and tracking
6. Sustainable industries
7. Cultural heritage and historic places permitting
8. Informing the public about the proposal
9. To suggests methods and measures to be included in the design to decrease the impacts.
10. To identify constraints associated with the mitigation measures recommended.

Methodology of EIA

EIA stands for a systematic process that evaluates the environmental effects of development measures before they are taken. The following steps make up the EIA approach.

1. project evaluation
2. Sussing
3. Alternatives are being considered.
4. Development initiative or project description
5. basic environment description
6. Identifying significant impacts
7. Potential consequences
8. Evaluation and significance assessment
9. Mitigation
10. The broader public's participation
11. EIS presented
12. Review

13. making choices
14. decision-making follow-up
15. Auditing